EDISON

IN THE

BOARDROOM

REVISITED

EDISON

IN THE

BOARDROOM

REVISITED

How
Leading Companies
Realize Value
from Their
Intellectual Property

Second Edition

SUZANNE S. HARRISON
AND PATRICK H. SULLIVAN

WILEY

John Wiley & Sons, Inc.

Published by John Wiley & Sons, Inc., Hoboken, New Jersey.

Published simultaneously in Canada

For general information on our other products and services or for technical support, please contact our Customer Care Department within the United States at (800) 762-2974, outside the United States at (317) 572-3993 or fax (317) 572-4002.

Wiley also publishes its books in a variety of electronic formats. Some content that appears in print may not be available in electronic formats. For more information about Wiley products, visit our web site at www.wiley.com.

Library of Congress Cataloging-in-Publication Data:

Harrison, Suzanne S.

    Edison in the boardroom : how leading companies realize value from their intellectual property / Suzanne S. Harrison, Patrick H. Sullivan. – 2nd ed.

      p.   cm.

    Prev. ed. entered under: Davis, Julie L.

    Includes bibliographical references and index.

    ISBN 978-1-118-00453-1 (cloth); ISBN 978-1-118-17012-0 (ebk);

    ISBN 978-1-118-17013-7 (ebk); ISBN 978-1-118-17014-4 (ebk)

      1. Corporations–Valuation.   2. Intellectual capital.   3. Research, Industrial–Economic aspects.   4. Technological innovations–Economic aspects.

I. Sullivan, Patrick H.   II. Davis, Julie L. Edison in the boardroom.   III. Title.

    HG4028.V3D38   2012

    658.4'038–dc23

                                               2011029931

Printed in the United States of America

10 9 8 7 6 5 4 3 2 1

We dedicate this book to all ICM Gathering members, past and present. Your individual and collective wisdom and experiences created the best practices and underlying principles that are the basis for this book. Through your willingness to openly share and build upon each other's ideas, you have contributed significantly to our community's understanding of how to successfully manage that most complex of company assets: intellectual property.

Good fortune is what happens when opportunity meets with planning. The value of an idea lies in the using of it.

If we all did the things we are really capable of doing, we would literally astound ourselves. . . .

—Thomas Alva Edison

Contents

Acknowledgments

The contents of this book represent a snapshot of the current state of understanding of the ICM Gathering companies as they continue the journey they began in 1995. At that time, seven companies met to share ideas about "Intellectual Capital" and how to manage it. The group has been meeting three times each year and continues to share its ideas on new and better ways to create and extract value from intangibles such as intellectual property. To fully acknowledge all of the people who contributed to the concepts and best practices in this book, we must thank everyone who has ever participated in a Gathering meeting, because each meeting inevitably produced counterintuitive insights into all aspects of intellectual property management.

Additionally we would like to thank the members of the Executive Forum for their insights into the emerging patent transaction marketplace and their assistance in standardizing the information required to conduct patent transactions more efficiently.

We are particularly indebted to two groups of people: the current membership of the ICM Gathering who defined and described the current best practices for IP management, and the company executives who took the time to be interviewed for this book from January through

April 2011. Their candid descriptions about how they and their companies applied the best practices or basic principles in everyday operations, as well as their successes and failures, deserve our special thanks: Seungho Ahn, Steve Baggott, Gary Bender, Scott Coonan, Mark Connolley, Kevin Donnolley, Arian Duijvestijn, Scott Frank, Harry Gwinnell, Jesper Kongstad, Ron Laurie, Allen Lo, Erik Oliver, Jim O'Shaughnessey, Ruud Peters, Gene Potkay, Mark Radcliffe, Kent Richardson, Elizabeth Sussex, and Mark Zdeblick.

In the course of developing ideas for this book we have talked with a number of colleagues whose perspectives have been particularly helpful in shaping and supporting our view of the art of intellectual property management. They include Sharon Oriel, John Raley, Bill Swirsky, Rob McLean, Rupert Mayer, Kate Spelman, Karol Denniston, and Eric Shih, Larry Lunetta, and Lila Klapman.

We would also like to thank Susan McDermott and Jennifer MacDonald for their patience and support in guiding us through the John Wiley & Sons process. Thanks also go to Alexandra Lajoux for recreating the "voice" of the first edition of *Edison in the Boardroom*. We would especially like to thank Julie Davis, without whom the IP Value hierarchy would never have come into being, and whose continued support throughout the past 10 years has been greatly appreciated.

And finally, thanks to our families for their support, suggestions, and words of encouragement, even during the times we missed family obligations and worked on weekends and holidays. Without their patience and understanding, this book would never have been born.

Chapter 1

Introduction

The lightbulb and its inventor, Thomas Alva Edison, have become synonymous with invention. When we think of a bright idea, we envision a lightbulb. When we think of prolific inventors, Edison usually tops the list. But the true legacy of Edison did not stop with invention; it expanded to include innovation—the subject of this book.

Invention is merely the conception of an idea—the start of a process that will eventually produce value. *Innovation*, by contrast, is the life of an idea. It begins with "invention" and ends with value that can be captured and demonstrated in financial statements and, yes, in the cash box. An invention becomes an innovation when it is successfully introduced into the marketplace. And this is true whether the "product" emerges as tangible goods or an intangible service.

It is innovation, not invention, that generates corporate profits and competitive advantage. Far too many companies focus solely on invention at the expense of devoting resources and attention to the full process of innovation.

Most companies are fascinated by invention—from proof of concept to launch. Much energy goes into creating an initial working version of a product, scaling it to achieve industrial levels of production, and creating and testing a beta version.

To some companies, it may seem that, at this point, the job is done. In truth, it is only beginning.

To extract commercial value from an invention, a company must do more. It must *innovate*, by creating the pipeline of business capabilities needed to transform the invention into a marketable product and positioning it in locations where the customer can obtain it. This means creating (or contracting for) the key business assets or capabilities needed to convert the invention into something a customer can buy. This may include manufacturing and distribution, advertising, financing, packaging, and even legal protection for the original idea and sometimes also for additional inventions that will support the creation of the eventual product.

For centuries, companies have converted ideas into profits by embedding their new concepts (legally protected or not) into products that are sold or bartered. In recent decades, however, the emergence of intangibles as important business assets has revolutionized the way companies get value out of their ideas. In addition to embedding an invention into a product to create value (classical innovation), ideas are licensed, sold, or bartered in their raw state. But for greater amounts of value, companies often link the invention to the firm's complementary capabilities, thus creating new and marketable innovations. In some cases, this value through innovation fails to recapture the original investment; in other cases it turns a profit; and in yet other instances it makes an ongoing fortune that can be shared all along a value chain.

So how are companies profiting from their ideas? In brief, they are deriving value through intellectual property (IP) management. But to do this requires a new mind-set. Intangible assets, much more than tangible ones, can be difficult to value and to measure. *Edison in the Boardroom*, first published in 2001, described the real-life experiences of companies at different levels of IP sophistication and how they manage their intellectual property for business value. When Davis and Harrison wrote the earlier edition of *Edison* a decade ago, they wanted to create a simple framework to measure the differences in how IP management is

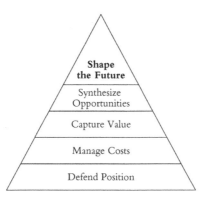

Figure 1.1   The Value Hierarchy

practiced by a range of companies. Ultimately, they identified five different levels of IP management that they had observed—from the primary need to defend a concept to more sophisticated use of IP to shape the future. They called this the Value Hierarchy (see Figure 1.1) and it is discussed later in this chapter and throughout this book.

The pyramid describes how companies used their IP portfolio to support the firm's business and what it was trying to accomplish. To learn best practices for companies residing at each level of the pyramid, Davis and Harrison turned to the ICM Gathering, a group founded in 1995 that focused on discovering how to get value out of a firm's intangibles.[1] The Gathering companies helped revise the descriptions of each level, discussed the processes involved, and eventually provided examples of best practices for companies at each level, based on their own applications of the principles of IP management, which they had evolved through The Gathering for themselves.

Why Update *Edison in the Boardroom?*

Over the decade since the original *Edison* was published, the ICM Gathering companies have continued to meet and discuss how to create and extract ever more value from their intangibles, particularly in the face of the rapidly changing business and IP environments.

Sharon Oriel, CEO of Talisker Consulting and a member of The Gathering since its inception, explains, "Gathering companies are able to share what they do to manage their patents, so that Gathering companies are able to learn from each other and yet no competitive advantages are lost by the sharing company. Why is that? The reason is that the 'what' is shared and discussed, but not the 'how.' Since each company needs to adapt the 'what' to their own company, each company is free to create a competitive advantage with how they implement the new IP process[es]."

But many of the best practices mentioned by Gathering members in the original *Edison* began to change. As the first decade of the new century progressed, significant changes began to appear, along with changes in the world of technology, such as cloud computing,[2] Skype, and the iPad. For their part, the grantors of intellectual property rights revolutionized their own technology through such innovations as the electronic Priority Document Exchange (PDX).[3] Gathering companies began to recognize that their IP management techniques were evolving to reflect the changing state of the IP and business worlds.

Eventually the Gathering companies began to discuss whether to update the original *Edison* book to reflect the current state of play. They decided to share their own experiences and observations as they related to the levels of IP management sophistication, and best practices associated with each new level.

Julie Davis's professional interests had shifted away from IP management toward images analysis in IP litigation. Suzanne Harrison turned to her ICM Gathering co-facilitator and long-time collaborator, Patrick Sullivan, and soon the new edition was under way. Originally seen as a cut-out-the-old-stuff and paste-in-the-new-stuff book, it soon became apparent that this would not be possible. The changes in the business and IP environments were too significant and their impact on IP management too great. A total update was needed.

This book retains the format of the original edition, as well as a small amount of its material. Over 85 percent of the content of this book is new:

- We've added a chapter describing the changes that have occurred in the environment within which IP is managed by companies in 2011 as compared with 2001.
- While we have retained the pyramid icon, the focus of each level has been updated to reflect the changes that have occurred in the IP management environment over the past decade.
- All of the best practices for each level have been upgraded or revised.

- The generic IP management system has been significantly updated to reflect the latest practices of Gathering companies.
- We've added a chapter that speaks directly to companies asking themselves what they should do if they aren't even sophisticated enough to qualify for the first level of the Edison pyramid.
- This book differentiates between invention and innovation and shows how Gathering companies are managing that distinction to benefit their companies.
- In the first edition, the focus for companies was largely inward; what they could and should do to match their IP management activity with what they wanted to accomplish. In *Edison Revisits the Boardroom* we show how IP-sophisticated companies are focused on using IP to gain strategic position outside of the company.
- In the first edition, optimizing the interaction between IP and R&D was simple and relatively direct. In *Edison Revisits the Boardroom,* a core premise of the future is that IP and R&D will need to become intertwined. This book discusses and shows examples of how companies use Open Innovation to expand their invention and innovation capabilities, as well as use it to improve the company's profit position.
- We've added several new Appendices:
  - Significant Developments in Intellectual Property Law in the Past 10 Years.
  - The Rise of Patent Aggregators.
  - An Update on IP Damages.
- In this book we have added a number of topics that have become part of the IP management set of capabilities for Gathering companies:
  - Determining the Context of the Future.
  - Influencing and Creating the Future.
  - Developing Make versus Buy Decision Processes.
  - IP Metrics and Reporting.
  - Managing IP Risk/Reward Trade-Offs.

There is, however, an important distinction about the new book that should be called out. *Edison in the Boardroom Revisited* is a book about patents. This does not imply that there is nothing new in either copyrights or trademarks; it is merely a reflection that the ICM Gathering has spent much of the past three years focusing on how changes in the patent ecosystem have affected their bottom lines and their need to create better processes to manage those impacts. But one important part of this book has not changed since our first edition: the history of how this book began.

A Brief History

The authors first became interested in the business value of intellectual property in 1987 after reading a research paper by Professor David Teece of the Haas School of Business at the University of California, Berkeley.[4] Even prior to Teece's work, it was common knowledge that patents, trademarks, and copyrights have value. But Teece's concept went further. His hypothesis that they have *additional* economic value beyond their defensibility was startling, as was Teece's concept of the steps companies could take to increase the amount of that value. It was to be seven more years until a few adventurous companies would begin methodically extracting economic value from their company's knowledge, know-how, and intellectual property.[5]

Historically, tangible assets held the greatest value for business and industry: cash, real estate, oil, gold, and so forth. But by the middle of the 1990s an invisible line was crossed and things that were *in*tangible came to be of greater value.

In October 1994, Tom Stewart of *Fortune* magazine coined the term intellectual capital (IC), which he defined as the intangible assets such as skill, knowledge, and information. In late 1994, The ICM Group, LLC, a consulting company founded by the authors, began contacting all the companies who were actively trying to manage their intangible assets. In January 1995, representatives from seven of these companies assembled for a meeting to share what their IC efforts entailed. At that first meeting, the group defined intellectual capital as "knowledge that can be converted to value." They also determined that IC has two main components: human capital (tacit knowledge—ideas we have in our heads) and intellectual assets (codified knowledge—ideas that have been codified in some manner). Within intellectual assets, there is a subset of ideas that can be legally protected, and these are called intellectual property (IP). See Figure 1.2.

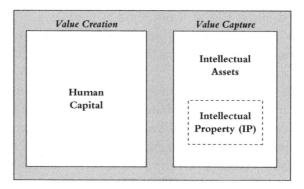

Figure 1.2 Intellectual Capital

The original group of seven companies that met in January 1995 has now grown to over 30 companies that meet three times a year to create, define, and benchmark best practices in the emerging area of ICM. This group is collectively known as the ICM Gathering. The Gathering has spent the past years working on creating and defining systems and processes for companies to routinely create, identify, and realize value from intellectual assets.

Early in its existence, The Gathering decided to share its lessons openly, reasoning that the more companies there were that practiced these lessons in practice, then the more companies there would be to learn from. To date the members of the ICM Gathering have produced five books (including this one) and more than four dozen published articles, all about capturing and realizing value from an organization's intellectual property.

This value is growing with each new generation. We all know that in-process research and development (R&D)—as well as the entire patent portfolio—has immense value to the firm, yet in accounting, value is not "accounted for" until it is realized or a transaction has occurred.

The businessperson's view of the world has been shaped largely by double-entry accounting, which was first created in 1494 by Luca Pacioli, an Italian monk. Believe it or not, this is fundamentally the same accounting system that is used by global corporations around the world today to calculate and report revenues, profits, and expenses, and make decisions about resource allocations, risk management, and investment returns. While accounting is very good at recording transactions that have occurred in the past, it is not good at predicting future revenue streams. In addition, accounting only records transactions, so financial statements routinely exclude ideas that have not yet manifested themselves in a transaction.

In recent years, the amount of company value attributable to intellectual capital has increased dramatically. In a study of thousands of nonfinancial companies over a 20-year period, Dr. Margaret Blair, of the Brookings Institute, reported a significant shift in the makeup of company assets. She studied all of the nonfinancial publicly traded firms in the Compustat database. In 1978, her study showed that 80 percent of the firms' value was associated with its tangible assets, with 20 percent associated with its intangible assets. In 10 years, by 1988, the makeup had shifted to 45 percent tangible assets and 55 percent intangible assets. By 1998, only 30 percent of the value of the firms studied was attributable to their tangible assets, while a stunning 70 percent was associated with the value of their intangibles.

This study, often cited as support for assertions about the increasing portion of a firm's market value associated with its intangibles, was prescient, but flawed.[6] Like many analysts of corporate value, Dr. Blair defines the value of a company's intangibles as the difference between its market value and the value of its tangible assets. But this definition treats IP as if it could be valued as an "asset." Our experience is different. We find that IP acts more like a mini-generator of revenue and income than it does as an asset. From our perspective, valuing IP as an asset is meaningless, whereas valuing it as a generator of value seems to more accurately reflect the kind of value it provides to the firm.[7] It is best to analyze this for oneself; the market is too volatile to make such a determination. We agree, however, with Dr. Blair that the portion of a firm's value associated with its intangibles has increased dramatically and persistently over the past four decades, and for this finding we owe her a debt of gratitude.

Intellectual Property: The Big Three-Plus

Patents

A patent is typically defined as a grant extended to the owner of an invention (the individual inventor, or an entity that owns the invention) that excludes others from making, using, or selling the invention, and includes the right to license others to make, use, or sell the invention. Patents are protectable under the U.S. Constitution, and under the Patent Cooperation Treaty of 1970, in Title 35 of the U.S. Code. Patent protection can be extended to inventions that are novel (new and original), useful, and not obvious. Some corporations have patentable inventions but choose to protect them as trade secrets, rather than filing for a patent.*

Patents may be issued for four general types of inventions/discoveries: compositions of matter, machines, man-made products (including design and bioengineering), and processing methods (including business processes). To obtain a patent, the inventor must send a model or a detailed description to the U.S. Patent and Trademark Office, which employs examiners who review applications. The average time between patent application and issuance is about 2.5 years, although the process may be much shorter or longer, depending on the situation.

Under current international trade law (as described in the most recent General Agreement on Tariffs and Trade), patents are issued for a nonrenewable period of 20 years measured from the date of application. Inventors being granted patents in the United States must pay maintenance fees. Federal courts have exclusive jurisdiction over disputes involving patents.

Trademarks

A trademark is the right to use a name associated with a company, product, or concept, as well as the right to use a symbol, picture, sound, or even smell associated with these factors. The mark can already be in use or be one that will be used in the future.

---

*A trade secret is "information, including a formula, pattern, compilation, program, device, method, technique, or process" that is kept a secret and that derives value from being kept secret. Many states have adopted the Uniform Trade Secrets law to govern this area.

(*Continued*)

A trademark may be assigned to a trade name, which is the name a company uses to operate its business. Trademarks may be protected by both federal statute under the Lanham Act, which is now part of Section 15 of the U.S. Code, and under a state's statutory and/or common law. Trademark status may be granted to unique names, symbols, and pictures, and also unique building designs, color combinations, packaging, presentation, and product styles (called trade dress), and even Internet domain names. Trademark status may also be granted for identification that does not appear to be distinct or unique, but that over time has developed a secondary meaning identifying it with the product or seller.

The owner of a trademark has the exclusive right to use it on the product it was intended to identify and often on related products. Service marks receive the same legal protection as trademarks but are meant to distinguish services rather than products. A trademark is indefinite in duration, so long as the mark continues to be used on or in connection with the goods or services for which it is registered, subject to certain defenses. Federally registered trademarks must be renewed every 10 years. Trademarks are protected under state law, even without federal registration, but registration is recommended. Most states have adopted a version of the Model Trademark Bill and/or the Uniform Deceptive Trade Practices Act.

Copyrights
A copyright is the right of ownership extended to an individual who has written or otherwise created a tangible or intangible work, or to an organization that has paid that individual to do the work while retaining possession of the work. Copyright protection grew out of protection afforded by the U.S. Constitution to "writings." Subsequent law (U.S. Copyright Act, U.S. Code in Title 17, Section 106) has extended this term to include works in a variety of fields, including architectural design, computer software,* graphic arts, motion pictures, sound recordings (for example, on audio compact discs and MP3 files), and videos. Any

---

*Uniform Trade Secrets Act, Section 1ff., 14 U.S.C.A. 541.

type of work may be copyrighted, as long as it is "original," and in a "concrete medium of expression." (Computer software, although intangible, is considered a concrete medium.)

A copyright gives the owner exclusive rights to the work, including right of display, distribution, licensing, performance, and reproduction. A copyright may also grant to the owner the exclusive right to produce (or license the production of) derivatives of the work. In general, a copyright lasts for the life of the owner, plus 70 years. "Fair use" of the work is exempt from copyright law. The fairness of use is judged in relation to a number of factors, including the nature of the copyrighted work, purpose of the use, size, and substantiality of the portion of copyrighted work used in relation to that work as a whole, and potential market for or value of the copyrighted work. Copyrights are protected under both state and federal law, with federal law superseding. A number of organizations promote the protection of intellectual property, including the World Intellectual Property Organization, which covers copyrights, patents, and trademarks.

The Edison Mind-Set

The growing emphasis on ideas is not new to the times. In Thomas Edison's era, the key inventions were related to the airplane, lightbulb, telegraph, telephone, and automobile. Today key inventions are emerging around the Internet, software, and business processes. Thomas Edison personified the "creative genius" of the era when he said (in a phrase captured by his colleague Francis Upton):

> Men are just beginning to propose questions and find answers, and we may be sure that no matter what question we ask, so long as it is not against the laws of nature, a solution can be found.[8]

The "we" here was no mere rhetorical device, but a new way of thinking. Thomas Edison is often romanticized as a maverick inventor—the creator of the lightbulb, the motion picture, the microphone, and myriad other technologies. Less well known is his invention of the modern research laboratory using teams of inventors.

To be sure, Edison will forever be the very symbol of brainpower. In his lifetime, he would obtain 1,093 patents, including one for the incandescent electric lamp—a prototype of the "lightbulb" that would come to symbolize the "bright" idea. Other patents included those for the phonograph, the microphone, and the motion picture projector—technologies that would shape a century. His years of invention came at the outset of an era. Starting in the late nineteenth century, the United States would experience a steady rise in patents that would continue to the present, boosted by innovations in telegraphy, electricity, automobiles, airplanes, synthetics, aerospace, and most recently, high technology including the new Internet economy.

But despite the brilliance of Thomas Edison's inventions, one might well say that his greatest contribution to society was not any particular discovery, but rather the creation of the world's first research laboratories—two laboratories, in fact, in Menlo Park and West Orange, New Jersey. As one source notes, his workshops were "forerunners of the modern industrial research laboratory, in which teams of workers, rather than a lone inventor, *systematically investigate a problem.*"[9] Edison, more than any other scientist of his day, knew that to generate ideas and successfully commercialize them required *sustained and methodical effort.*

The Lightbulb: A Brief History

The lightbulb may symbolize the quick flash of invention, but it also represents the long, slow process of bringing an idea to the marketplace. Known technically as the incandescent lamp, a lightbulb is simply a glass bulb enclosing an electrically heated filament that emits light. As simple as it may sound, this object was very difficult to produce, and had a significant impact on society.

Before Thomas Edison began working on the lightbulb, 20 inventors before him had similar insights, but nothing significant came of their efforts. For example, in 1802, Humphry Davy passed an electric current through a platinum wire and lit it up, but he did not protect or pursue this invention. In 1845,

American J. W. Star received an English patent for a "continuous metallic or carbon conductor intensely heated by the passage of electricity for the purpose of illumination." Building on Star's invention, Joseph Swann experimented with lamps between 1848 and 1860, but never produced anything practical until 1877, when he renewed his efforts at exactly the same time that Thomas Edison was turning his attention to electricity.

Edison was by far the most persistent of this line of inventors. He experimented with a variety of materials—including mandrake bamboo from Japan—before he finally hit on a solution: the use of a filament made of carbonized cotton sewing thread. Edison patented this procedure, but lost a patent infringement case initiated by Swan. In order to make peace, the two men formed the Edison and Swan United Electric Light Company Limited in 1883. The company acquired several other companies and renamed itself Edison Electric. It eventually merged with another company, renaming itself General Electric, or GE, in 1892.

Interestingly, it was a GE scientist who finally made the commercial breakthrough. Irving Langmuir tackled a persistent problem with the lightbulb—the tendency of the filament to crumble, and the bulb to blacken, after a short period of use. After three solid years of experimentation, Langmuir solved the problem in GE labs, and won the Nobel Prize for his discovery.[*]

[*]This history is based on a variety of sources, including the Edison books cited in other notes to this chapter. The portion on Langmuir comes from Robert Buderi, *Engines of Tomorrow: How the World's Greatest Companies Are Using Their Research Labs to Win the Future* (New York: Simon & Schuster, 2000), 76.

The level of effort seen in Edison's laboratories continues in America's companies today. The authors work with clients who hunger to find new sources of value—but where? Companies have already been reengineered, reorganized, and restructured. Their workforce has been downsized, right-sized, and empowered. Their inventory is just-in-time. Their core competencies have been benchmarked and noncore functions outsourced. And companies have streamlined their factory operations, introduced many quality initiatives, and partnered with suppliers, customers, and communities. How then can more value be created?

To quote Edison's optimistic phrase again, "*no matter what question we ask, so long as it is not against the laws of nature, a solution can be found.*" In our work together, we share the mind-set of Thomas Edison. We agree with him that inventiveness will never end, but more important, we agree that it is hard work and perseverance that fuels the continuing flow of invention. This is a message that companies today can take to heart as they develop, protect, and enhance their intellectual assets day in and day out—for months, for years, and for generations.

The answer for our clients then and now has been a rediscovery of intellectual assets—current and future, legally protected or not. Intellectual assets that are legally protected are covered by patent, trademark, and copyright laws, as well as laws protecting trade secrets. Intellectual assets that are not protected by such laws include company know-how, culture, and contracts—all clearly very important to any company, yet not protectable.

The Enhanced Business Reporting Framework[10] an initiative of the American Institute of Certified Public Accountants features this checklist of assets and competencies:

- Key processes
- Customer satisfaction
- People
- Innovation
- Supply chain
- Information and technology
- Intellectual property
- Financial assets
- Physical assets

With the exception of the last three items, few of these are protectable—yet they clearly contribute to company value.[11]

In our joint work with companies around the world, we have developed an appreciation for the best practices in the management and capitalization of intellectual assets—and how those practices yield results that affect both profits and shareholder value. From working behind the scenes, we know from experience that the real value in intellectual assets lies not only in the inspiration that gives it life, but also in the perspiration that fully develops it and captures its value. That is why Edison's dedication to innovation appeals to us.

Marching in step with Edison, we believe that inventions will continue to stream forth, and that each and every one of them will require *hard work* to bring into full value. Our own systematic work in investigating extracting value from patents (as a prototypical type of intellectual property) has led us to study their "sweat" component—the diligent, methodical work of *defending ownership, controlling costs, extracting profits, integrating with other aspects of a business, and, finally, mapping out a future strategy.* We have identified the best practices of leading companies that relate to the realization of value from their intellectual assets.

We have found, though, that benchmarking best practices without any regard for the underlying culture of the firm can be problematic. For example, many firms want to make money from licensing fees. We have met many IP executives who have been told by their CEOs, "If our competitor can get $1 billion in licensing fees, by golly, so can we," and then in the next breath have also said, "but don't come back here and tell me I need to hire any more lawyers!" The point, of course, is that it took a substantial investment in both R&D and legal resources to generate that $1 billion royalty stream. Most CEOs are not prepared to make a similar investment. So we realized that it was important for companies to understand where they were in their awareness of the management of intellectual property, and to create a way for them to articulate where they want to be, and then identify best practices to allow them to get there.

The Value Hierarchy

From that research we have developed an appreciation for the best practices in the management of intellectual assets, especially intellectual property, and how those practices yield results that affect both profits and shareholder value. The collective learnings of the Gathering companies are the foundation for the best practices of this book. But a raw list of best practices is relatively difficult for new companies to integrate into their existing processes and decision systems, and therefore we presented the Value Hierarchy (previously shown in Figure 1.1).

Think of the Value Hierarchy as a pyramid with five levels. Each level represents a different expectation the company has about the contribution that its IP function should be making to the corporate goals. Each higher level on the pyramid represents the increasing demands placed upon the IP function by the executive team and the board of directors. Like building blocks, each higher level relies on the foundation of the lower levels. Mastery of the practices, characteristics, and activities of the prior levels builds the foundation for greater increases in shareholder value at the next level. The more one builds on intellectual property on Level One, the better one is able to enhance the value of all intellectual assets—and more broadly, intellectual capital—at the higher levels.[12]

- Level One of the Value Hierarchy is the "Defend Position" level. If a corporation owns an invention (such as a great business concept), it can prevent competitors from using the asset. By staking a claim on its valuable intellectual properties, a company builds a base from which to obtain more value from them. This is the most fundamental of the IP functions, which is why it is at the base of our pyramid. At this level, the IP function provides a patent shield to protect the company from litigation. By stockpiling patents, companies can shield themselves from litigation because they may be able to negotiate cross-licenses rather than go to court. The IP function of companies involved heavily in this level tends to be run by the company's intellectual property counsel. Companies at this level generally view IP as a legal asset.
- Level Two is the "Manage Costs" level, in which companies focus on how to reduce the costs of filing and maintaining their IP portfolios. The focus also shifts more toward managing IP-related risk while still maintaining cost control. Finally, conversations around innovation preferences (make versus buy) should begin in this level. Well-executed strategies in this area can save the company millions of dollars annually. Companies focusing on this activity may still put an attorney in charge of the function, but the attorney is more likely to have a background in business. Intellectual property is still viewed primarily as a legal asset.
- Level Three of the Value Hierarchy is the "Capture Value" level. Companies reach this level when they are interested in putting IP

on the management scorecard. Having learned how to control many of their patent-related costs, companies at this level turn their attention to more proactive strategies that can generate millions of dollars of additional value, while continuing to trim costs. Passing from the previous levels of activity to this one requires a *major change* in a company's attitude—and even organization. In Level Three companies, IP may have its own function, and the individual in charge may even be Chief Intellectual Property Officer (CIPO). It is at this level that companies begin to view IP as a business asset, rather than just a legal asset.

- Level Four is the "Synthesize Opportunities" level. In this level company management has grasped the power of using IP for a range of business roles. Companies at this level recognize that IP is truly a strategic asset for the firm, and CIPOs look to more sophisticated IP management processes. A more systematic process to measure IP risk/reward trade-offs is implemented. Clarity around the relationship of invention to innovation is discussed broadly within the company. Here the focus is on the process, not just on IP.

- Level Five, the final level, is the "Shape the Future" level. These companies, having reached this level, are looking outside themselves and into the future. In this level, the IP function, having already become deeply ingrained in the company, takes on the challenge of identifying future technology trends and consumer preferences. It anticipates technological revolutions and actively seeks to position the corporation as a leader in its field by acquiring or developing the IP that will be necessary to protect the company's margins and market share and by placing patent options in the future. Finally, companies at this level recognize that they need to utilize group dynamics to both predict and influence possible futures for the firm.

Few, if any, corporations *in the world* have mastered all five levels and captured the maximum value from their intellectual assets. *Every* corporation has room for improvement. *Every* corporation has an opportunity to increase its value by strengthening and building on its intangible assets.

Keep in mind that each level on this pyramid serves as the foundation or building block for the levels above it. Many, if not most, companies may actually be engaging in activities from several different levels simultaneously. These same companies, though, can benefit by candidly assessing where they stack up compared to others. It is not a bad thing to recognize that your company may only be functioning in the bottom levels. Indeed, there are a number of very large and very sophisticated companies at Levels One and Two. Companies at these levels can make a difference in their IP management and improve shareholder value in a noticeable way. Yet many can do better.

Moving from one level to the next in the Value Hierarchy requires discipline, organization, and leadership. And it requires a road map to avoid the mistakes made by similar organizations in the past. It is important for a company to know the best practices used by other IP leaders, both inside the company's industry as well as in other industries. By mastering all five levels, a company can get the most out of all its intellectual capital—including, perhaps most importantly, its patents.

In this book, we focus on intellectual property, especially patents.

Of all types of intellectual property, the quintessential one is the patent. Indeed, it bears the very name of public protection. The term *patent* derives from *litterae patentes*, which means something that is disclosed, rather than secret. By publishing or rendering "patent" an invention, the inventor protects his or her rights to it. The patent is also the most common form of intellectual property, and as we say, "is the most tangible of the intangibles." Also, the protection it grants is arguably the strongest.

The Intellectual Property Management System

To fully understand the Value Hierarchy, we need to see how companies systematically manage and extract value from their intellectual assets. We call this the Intellectual Property Management System (IPMS). Figure 1.3 depicts a generic IPMS as now visualized by the Gathering companies.

Though no one company uses a system identical to the one shown below, the Gathering companies have agreed that if they were to start all over again, they would each likely design a system with the components described in the box below. In the chapters to follow we focus on each

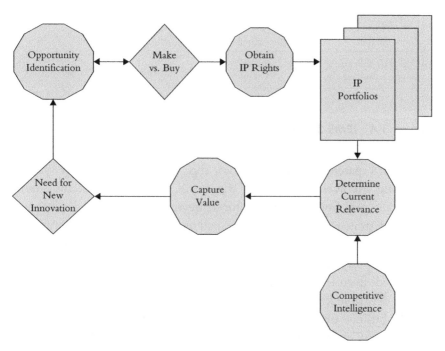

Figure 1.3   Generic IPMS

of these components as they relate to the best practices detailed for each level of the hierarchy.

Opportunity Identification

All firms have their own approach and method for developing new or innovative ideas that create value. For many technology companies this process is housed in an R&D activity; service companies, on the other hand, often have a creativity department; still others rely on their employees in the field to produce innovative ideas. Whatever the firm's source of new inventions, Opportunity awaits.

Opportunity Identification is one of the most important parts of the IPMS. It comprises four individual steps (see Figure 1.4).

Step 1: Update (Renew) Understanding of the Current Business Plan   It is important for decision-makers in the patenting process to be completely up to date on the firm's current business direction. Typically,

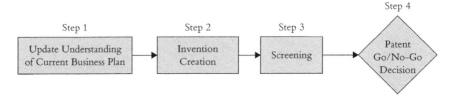

Figure 1.4 IPMS Steps

the firm's patent committee does this periodically, usually yearly. Updating involves a review of the firm's mission, vision, long-term objectives, and business strategy for achieving them. Once the business plan and strategy are verified, the patent committee can identify any elements or initiatives that could benefit from the kind of support intellectual property can provide. Looking broadly at the kind of support the firm needs from IP, one often finds that it may be summarized into three to five definable kinds of value sought from intellectual property. When specific business opportunities have been identified, and the kinds of value the company seeks to obtain from any IP that is to be created, one can then define the specific kind of IP needed (e.g., patent, copyright, trademark), as well as the specific characteristics and protections that must be provided by the new piece of IP.

Step 2: Invent (Create an Invention)   Once it has been determined which aspects of the business plan require support from IP and why, this information may be turned over to the people in the organization who have responsibility for invention. For companies whose invention function resides in R&D, or for companies with a creativity function, the management of these units takes on the task of identifying the desired kinds of inventions. But for other kinds of companies, those where creativity and ideation comes from employees generally within the firm, broader engagement may be needed. Sometimes these firms convene "invention disclosure" or "ideation" events, where employees gather, usually informally, and are asked to fill out some kind of form. These forms, often called "invention disclosures" capture a raw idea and the individual's thoughts about how that idea may be used to create value for the firm.

However it is accomplished, the result of the Invention Creation step is a number of invention disclosures the IP attorney and the patent committee may consider.

Step 3: Screening (Pick and Choose among Inventions) Many of the disclosed inventions will inevitably not be suitable for action by the company, and these need to be culled. The process for narrowing down the list of inventions usually involves several sets of screens. The first, and in some ways the most straightforward, is to determine whether the idea is capable of being converted into intellectual property. Many of the ideas will not meet the criteria for patent-ability, and others may not provide the protection desired through copyright or trademark. The second set of screens concerns the potential business value of the invention to the company; would investing in a patent on the idea provide the kind of value that the company needs. The third set of screens involves the technical desirability of the idea. Here the technology people weigh-in to determine whether the idea has technical merit, even if it has potential business value.

Step 4: Decide (Make a Patent Go/No-Go Decision) At this step in the Opportunity Identification Process the company (usually via its patent committee) must decide which of the surviving ideas of inventions are of sufficient merit to warrant investing in intellectual property protection. For each company this is a straight-up financial decision. Is the idea worth the expense of investment in protection, and perhaps subsequent commercialization?

The Make versus Buy Decision

Once the company's patent committee has a list of the ideas or inventions it has decided to protect, the next choice to consider is whether to make or buy—whether such a patent is to be developed and prosecuted by the company itself ("make" the patent), or whether it is preferable to go outside the firm to acquire the needed protection ("buy" the patent). The patent committee is faced with three alternative outcomes for their decision:

- Proceed with internal creation of the appropriate IP.
- Buy pre-existing IP from an external source.
- Commission an external source to create the IP under contract.

Make

- *Internal Invention*: Companies deciding to "make" their own patented technology first must ensure that they have the ability to develop the technology to the degree of sufficiency that is needed. Secondly, the firm must ensure that the invention meets the Patent and Trademark Office (PTO) standards for patentability. And, third, the firm must ensure that the prospective patented technology is at least consistent with the company's internal policies concerning patentability.

Buy

- *External Invention*: Companies deciding to have an external party create the technology must define the technology to be created. In addition, they must ensure that they can obtain unencumbered patent rights to the technology as part of their transaction agreement with the outside technology developer.
- *External Purchase*: In some cases the existing technology is already patented and available for purchase from another entity. When the company identifies such a circumstance, and then moves toward a purchase, it must also ensure that it is able to obtain the unencumbered patent rights to the technology as part of the transaction.

Obtaining the IP Rights

Following the decision to make or buy the needed IP protection, the organization will proceed down one of the three paths identified above. For each patent sought, the company's intent is to manage one of the three processes identified previously in order to produce the desired patent and insert it into the portfolio. See Figure 1.5.

Managing the IP Portfolios

Once a new patent or other piece of IP has been inserted into its respective portfolio, the IP manager becomes responsible for its administrative

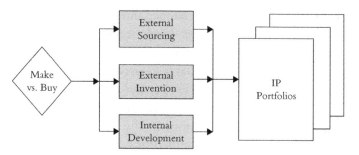

Figure 1.5   One of Three Paths

maintenance and for its intended use in support of the business. The first activity is purely administrative in nature and is usually turned over to the administrative staff. This activity involves the payment of all maintenance fees, along with information updates and the handling of requests for patent information.

The second activity is another story. Managing the IP portfolios for business value can be a complex activity, requiring a number of pieces of auxiliary information about the patent and its intended use for the firm. Here an electronic database is usually helpful for the IP manager. The database, in addition to containing all of the appropriate administrative information about each patent should also contain information about the patent and its relationship to the company's business. It may, for example, include information about the products or services the patent is intended to protect, the technology family to which the patent belongs, the business unit(s) with an interest in the protection provided by the patent, and so forth.

Portfolio management also implies that the IP manager will make routine reports about the portfolio's contents, its aging, its gaps vis-à-vis the company's desired protection, and information about the pace and content of the company's patent acquisition process.

Determining Relevance

Determining the relevant value of a patent involves two steps. The first step is to match the piece of IP with the firm's business strategy, tactics, and product/market mix. The second step is to quantify the amount of value it expects the innovation to provide.

The relevant value may have changed due to market conditions that have changed since the patent was developed and/or granted. For this reason, the effective IP management system will include an ongoing competitive intelligence activity that is focused on competitor patents.[13] While competitive assessments in business are commonplace, the competitive assessment contemplated here is one that is focused on the intellectual assets of the competition. In the case of technology companies, that focus might be on a competitor's technology as well as on its portfolio of patents.

Once a patent makes the grade as relevant and valuable, then the firm has the information it needs to capture the value it secured through the patent.

Value Capture

The Value Capture process is a natural follow-on to the preceding step. While firms have many ways to capture value from their patents, the following lists some of the most commonly used methods:

- Productize the patent: Use the patent to protect new product features.
- Monetize the patent: Obtain revenue directly from the use of the patent in a license or other value-generating use.
- Litigate the patent: Use the patent defensively as a deterrent to entities seeking to litigate and/or use the patent offensively in litigation.
- Positioning: Use the patent for competitive blocking, to create barriers to competitive entry and to enhance company reputation.

The Need for New Innovation

Sometimes in the course of innovation a company realizes that an existing invention needs another new invention to make it more marketable or more useful to the firm. In this case, the question is, What new invention may be needed? This becomes another input to the "Opportunity Identification" phase of the IPMS.

Every firm involved in extracting value from its intangible assets inevitably goes through the steps outlined earlier, each in its own way. One of the great challenges of IP management is how to create a system that works for each company according to its particular circumstances.

Summary

How exactly can a company convert its intellectual assets—particularly intellectual property—into the greatest value over time? In our consulting careers the authors have been privileged to meet individuals who are clearly "ahead of their time" when it comes to realizing value from their companies' innovations and ideas. As mentioned earlier, we have learned much by working with the members of the ICM Gathering. This book contains a collection of their learnings, along with success stories of other leading companies we have encountered in our work with clients who were striving to do a better job in leveraging and monetizing their intellectual assets.

Like Edison, the ICM Gathering practitioners are at the forefront of this value realization revolution. Many of the individuals we interviewed had a mandate to find value within a company that had already been mined for such gold. Most were expected to fail, but many succeeded. Like Thomas Edison, and like the companies he founded, the companies featured in this book exemplify the value of sustained, collective effort. It was this kind of effort that would eventually enable Edison to create and realize value from his innovations, showing that the place for value creation and realization is not only the laboratory but also the boardroom.

In the following pages, we will help you use a forward-looking yet methodical approach worthy of the Man from Menlo Park. For the remainder of this book, we authors, accompanied by the spirit of Thomas Edison, will travel with you as we build a Value Hierarchy for your company's intellectual assets. So turn the page to take the next step of the journey.

Chapter 2

The Changing Environment for IP Management

The previous edition of this book revived the legacy of Thomas Edison at a time when corporate leaders were just beginning to recognize the need for true innovation—the importance of managing intellectual property for business value. In the 10 intervening years, as boardrooms have pursued this goal, they have faced significant changes in the global business ecosystem all affecting—and affected by—IP. These include revolutionary developments in legal, judicial, economic, and management domains. In this chapter we highlight a decade's worth of the most important transformations from the perspective of operating companies managing their intellectual property, for business value—all based on ICM Gathering experience. These changes set the table for the subsequent discussions about current best practices for each level of the Edison Hierarchy.

We have identified some major changes that have affected the ways in which Gathering company managers view intellectual property, and the ways in which they manage it.

The Rise of the NPE (Nonpracticing Entity)

An NPE is an entity (or individual) that is attempting to monetize a patent asset or patent portfolio without making or selling product(s) covered by the patent(s). NPEs can arise for a number of reasons:

- The patented technology is too early for a market.
- The patented technology did not result in a saleable product.
- The patented technology is an alternative to a current or evolving standard.
- The company ran out of money before the product could be completed.
- The company never received sufficient funding to move forward.
- The patent holder is a university.

Although such situations have existed since the era of Edison, they have become more common in recent years due to the rise of a new type of NPE.[1] Although at least 11 different types of NPEs have been identified,[2] they can be boiled down to two:

1. An NPE that created the patented invention, whether the invention came from an individual inventor or as part of a company or university, and is looking to monetize it.
2. An NPE that did not create the patented invention, but has acquired the patent for monetization purposes.

The first type of NPE is nothing new. Perhaps the most famous NPE in this category is Jerome H. Lemelson (1923–1997), who held more than 600 patents yet never manufactured products. By licensing his patents, he reportedly made over $1 billion from his inventions.

What is new, however, is the concept of firms buying patent assets with the express intent of monetizing via litigation or the threat of litigation. The NPE exploits a situation in which innovation is so dense that it is no longer possible to release a product in the market without infringing on a number of patents (semiconductors is a good example).

NPEs mastering this approach include firms like Intellectual Ventures, Acacia, Altitude Capital, and Round Rock, and individuals such as Ronald Katz. In all cases, it basically comes down to money: NPEs have figured out an arbitrage opportunity they can exploit in the patent world.

This outcome of litigation as a business model is often blamed on NPEs, but operating companies are the first link in the chain. Many operating companies sold patents to NPEs, which then asserted rights against other operating companies—including competitors of the companies that sold the NPE the rights. Also, operating companies are often quick to settle with NPEs, which in turn provides the NPEs money for more patent acquisitions and further assertions. For more on the impact of NPEs in the IP ecosystem, please see Appendix B, "The Rise of Patent Aggregators."

Technology Convergence

Technologies and markets are converging more so now than ever in the past. For example, smart phones demonstrate the convergence of communication technologies, information technologies, and computer technologies. Technologically, they combine semiconductor technology, computing, LED display, social networking technology, geolocation, handset technology, telephony, and camera, to name a few. This means that companies that have heretofore not been technology or business competitors find themselves vying for ownership of patent assets to maintain competitive advantage in the new product market for smart phones.

In the past, before the emergence of these converged products, technologies, and markets, companies minimized risk by owning or otherwise controlling the patented technologies necessary to maintain their competitive advantage. Now, companies caught up in converging technology situations are finding that they have neither the time nor the resources to acquire the patents needed to ensure their future technology paths. So what do they do?

It is too early in the converging technology phenomenon to know what are the best solutions. Nevertheless, it appears we will need to rethink the concept of owning and controlling patented technology as the path toward ensuring future technology development. It may be that companies will find themselves moving toward a circumstance of alliances and relationships to enable access to patents that companies need when they need them.

The Arrival of the Chief Intellectual Property Officer (CIPO)

The discovery of intellectual property as a valuable asset with derivative value brought with it a new perspective on how companies might manage it. In the past, the individual usually responsible for the organization's IP was often an attorney who reported to the Chief Legal Officer or General Counsel. The attorney's job was to defend existing patents, not to ensure the development or acquisition of new ones. But for firms where IP has become a strategic driver, the IP function may move to a Chief Intellectual Property Officer (CIPO) who oversees all of the firm's IP activities and who reports directly to the CEO, as part of the "C-Suite." These firms have come to realize the power of IP and are increasingly pulling together under one manager all of their IP activities—portfolio administration, IP litigation, IP in mergers and acquisitions, IP licensing, and IP monetization in general. The need for this kind of centralized overview and management of the firm's IP endeavors is likely to grow as corporate leaders become more aware of intellectual property as a driver of corporate value. Many, if not most, of the individuals filling this position will be people with extensive business experience along with some understanding of the legal aspects of intellectual property.

Patents as an Investment Option

Many executives and financial officers think of intellectual property as an investment. But experienced CIPOs realize that it is an *option* on an investment—and, very much like a stock option, may lose or gain value based on the "market" for the invention. The difference between these two scenarios is significant. In most cases, a company creates a patent in anticipation that it will be used some time in the future. The future use may be for protection, or revenue generation, cost avoidance, or strategic positioning. It is often the case that one or more of these future anticipated uses of a patent fails to come about. But, if it does come about, the patent option is called and the patent assumes an often-significant amount of value through its use.

For example, a company is considering a strategic move into Asia. The long-term plan is to license the manufacturing rights to one of its popular products to companies in specific Asian countries. It decides to patent its manufacturing process in these countries to pave the way for the change. This will secure the company's rights to the technology in these countries in case it does expand there. But shortly after the company files the application, and before the strategic move could be initiated, a global recession hits and the company scraps its expansion plans. As a result, the patents, which could have been extremely valuable had the original strategy been executed, are now not worth very much to their owner; the "option" that the patents represented to their owner had expired.

Another example involves a company that manufactures and sells popular retail electronic products. In order to remain competitive, the company must anticipate customer demand and plan for a variety of new products. Its practice is to patent the key features of potential new products long before they are actually introduced into the market. But, if market tastes change, or new or disruptive technologies arise during the period before their patents issue, then the anticipated products may not be attractive in the marketplace, and the company may well decide not to introduce them. In this case, any option the company bought by creating the patent on product features becomes less valuable to them if the market opportunity for those products becomes moot. Although less valuable to the originating company, these patents could have considerable value to someone else, and therefore may be worthwhile pursuing.

For many companies, the value of the patents in their portfolio may be segmented into three groups. The first is the group of very valuable patents—the ones that drive strategic value (as defined by the firm). The second is a group of moderately valuable patents—the patents that protect and provide value for products and services the company is currently using in its business. Finally, the third contains those patents that no longer have value for the firm.

The first segment of the portfolio, the very valuable patents, typically comprises less than 5 percent of the total number of company patents. The second segment, the moderately valuable group of patents, most often comprises up to 70 percent of the company's patents. The remainder of patents—which can be up to half of a firm's patents—comprise those representing an "expired option", no longer having value for the firm.

Common sense might suggest that the value of patents in an organization's portfolio is distributed normally (like a bell-shaped curve), but experience has shown that it isn't; it follows a lognormal curve (see Figure 2.1). Patents are placed on the curve starting with the most valuable ones located at the intersection of the x- and y-axes. Each less valuable patent then follows in a parade from left to right on the axis. When we add the relative amounts of value associated with each patent, the result is the lognormal curve form shown in the Figure 2.1.

There are several interesting things to observe about this value distribution. The first is that there are only a small number of patents in the typical portfolio that have high value to the organization; as mentioned, probably fewer than 5 percent of the total. These patents are often considered to be the company's crown jewels, and are to be carefully tended and protected. The second thing one may notice about

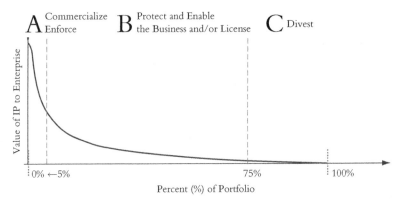

Figure 2.1 Lognormal Curve

the curve is the "saddle" shape in its middle. The saddle is where one finds the patents that are typically in operational use, forming the bulk of the company's operationally useful patents. As noted, this portion of the value distribution contains up to 70 percent of the patents. As one's eye moves to the right, the curve levels out and begins a persistent decline. This portion of the curve (from 25 to 50 percent of the patents) contains the patents that, while once useful to the organization, are no longer of value. They are candidates for pruning, or monetization.

The Globalization of Business

Although the movement toward business globalization began decades ago, the extent and pace of international trade has accelerated during the past decade. Companies in the developed world (traditionally identified as the United States, Europe, and Japan) seek access to new markets as well as low-cost labor abroad—although high unemployment at home is casting a pall on global outsourcing. Countries in the less-developed world (for example, in the poor countries of Africa and Latin America) are seeking jobs, investment, and a higher standard of living for their people. Countries in the middle—the so-called BRIC countries (Brazil, Russia, India, and China)—are industrializing rapidly, moving away from economies based on producing products created elsewhere to creating, producing, and distributing their own technology-based products into worldwide markets.

The 2011 earthquake and tsunami in Japan is a good example of how globalization has affected the world ecosystem. Japanese suppliers have been slow in ramping up production stopped by the earthquake, which has caused slow sales in the United States and around the world for cars, consumer electronics, and more. More and more global economies are interconnected, and a disruption in one country can have dramatic effects around the globe.

Patents and Politics: National IP Policy

National governments have now recognized the power of IP as an important tool in trade negotiations. We routinely see newspaper headlines discussing the impact of IP on healthcare, trade negotiations, and even the running of government communications networks (as in the dispute over BlackBerry technology, *NTP vs. Research in Motion [RIM]* case. This case was settled out of court for $612.5 million after the Canadian government took the side of RIM to ensure that a potential injunction did not occur[3]). In the United States alone, Congress has been involved in the patent reform debate for the past half decade. As of June 1, 2011, the America Invents Act of 2011 had received a favorable report out of committee and seemed likely to be legislated into law.[4] Additionally, the current patent backlog and the need for an increased USPTO budget to clear the backlog and modernize the patent office has also been discussed and unfortunately denied by Congress as well. In Europe, governmental influences can be seen in the debate over creating a European patent (as opposed to each European country requiring their own). Debates involving job losses and sovereign decision issues have routinely stalled this decision.

What is perhaps most interesting is that government leaders regularly cite the need for increased invention in order to maintain global competitiveness and then do nothing to enable the underlying IP system to handle any increased IP demand.

The Worldwide Patent Backlog*

Today there is a backlog of patent applications in patent offices worldwide. I'd like to give you my perspective on what I believe is the cause of this problem and then I'd like to talk about what we are doing to resolve the issue.

I believe there are two primary causes for the backlog problem. First and foremost, individuals and organizations are simply using the patent system more. This is actually good news. Industry is investing in the future and the world is evolving out of a classical economy into the knowledge economy. But when one examines the phenomenon a bit further, one finds that the *balance* of patenting has changed, and those changes mirror global

*Contributed by Jesper Kongstad, Director General, Danish Patent and Trademark Office.

economic development. For example, there are now more industrialized countries in the world and the new entrants into this classification are coming up to speed with more and more new patents.

The second cause of the backlog is more complex. It is natural for each country or regional patent system to favor its own principles and values. However, if you boil down the differences you soon recognize that they are based on national favoritism; we have ours and others have their own.

It is obvious that as more patents are exercised worldwide, applications must be examined multiple times in order to be issued in several countries or regions, and therefore the total capacity to examine and grant patents will be diminished.

Now let's look at some secondary issues that contribute to the problem. The public sector has ignored the growing backlog, in part because each jurisdiction is unwilling to give up its respective positions on minor details in the patent granting process. Consequently, they have been reluctant to cooperate in substantively harmonizing patent law.

The situation can be described as two trains rapidly approaching each other on the same track. The first train is the average survival time of patents. In Europe, it has been declining over time, having decreased from about 14 years, 10+ years ago, to about nine years for certain industries at present. The other train coming up the track is the average processing time in patent offices. The average in Europe has been about five years, but it is creeping upward to six or seven years. As a result, the window for the use of a granted patent (and therefore its presumed economic value) has diminished substantially because of these two factors.

So what is being done to turn this problem around? There are actually a large number of initiatives underway to solve the problem. Patent offices around the world have been hiring more patent examiners, in order to increase the throughput of their patent examination and granting processes. Unfortunately,

(*Continued*)

training new examiners takes time, so we can't expect to see results rapidly, but we can expect to see them over time. Also, patent offices are working diligently to eliminate inefficiencies wherever they can be found, and updating their systems and processes in order to increase throughput.

Another set of initiatives surrounds the Patent Prosecution Highway (PPH), a system invented by the United States Patent and Trademark Office (USPTO) and Japanese Patent Office to minimize the reexamination time of a patent already granted by another entity. The PPH is based on the idea that there is no reason why one should completely reexamine a patent if it has already been issued by another jurisdiction. The second office could, for example, review any issues related to national law, and otherwise simply build on the work already completed by the first office. This initiative is progressing, although slowly, as jurisdictions are resisting giving up control.

Other work-share arrangements are being explored and initiated. In Europe, the European Patent Office (EPO) is the focal point for working with national jurisdictions to work share. We are hoping to develop methods and processes that can be shared with others.

I can't say how long it will take to make the changes I've indicated, but it is clear that we are all now aware that we have to solve the backlog problem and to do so in a way that uses the worldwide PTO resources in a more efficient manner. No jurisdiction can afford to break the bank to solve the problem by itself, so finding shared solutions appears to offer our best chance for success. I am confident that we will get it done, although how long it will take is still uncertain.

The Need for Further Harmonization of IP Law

The business world has become largely international in scope. The globalization of business is also important in the IP context because intellectual property is a *national* right, not an international one.

A company has to have a patent in several national jurisdictions in order to have coverage for the scope of their international business; for example, they may require a U.S. patent, a Japanese patent, and a European patent. Because of this, the differences in patent law from one national jurisdiction to the next are becoming more apparent. Combine this situation with the global nature of the Internet and it is difficult to determine who has jurisdiction over an IP issue. For example, if the IP issue is raised in the UK but the servers are located in the Cayman Islands and the company resides in the United States, who has jurisdiction?

The Rise of China as a Patenting Powerhouse

China in decades past was known as a badland of counterfeiting and patent infringement, but a new China is underway. China is a special case, both because of its immense size and also because it is involved in its own version of manifest destiny and national development. It has made tremendous social and political changes over the past decade toward bringing the entire country into the twenty-first century. China's assertive development policy involves using all of the means it can muster to help with modernization, industrialization, technological invention, and commercial innovation.

The Chinese are following the same pattern of industrial and intellectual property development as both Europe and the United States. At first they were quite critical of the intellectual property system as being unfair to less developed countries. They then largely ignored it and freely copied Western inventions, imitating the products being created, manufactured, and sold in the developed nations. In recent years, as China has become capable of invention and innovation, the Chinese have become interested in the patent system as protecting their own interests. They are now a part of the system and no longer outside it.

Understanding the importance of patent protection, China has spent the past 10 years creating IP awareness among its enterprises, along with a new set of laws and judicial system to bring it into alignment with the rest of the world regarding IP. Its system for enforcing court decisions is still evolving and the battle to deter would-be IP infringers and copyright pirates still rages on, but China very clearly understands that its future relies on transitioning from a manufacturing-based country to an innovation-based one.

Western concerns that the Chinese might use their judicial system in a manner that is predatory toward foreigners have largely been laid to rest. Recent reports suggest that 80 percent of the patent cases filed in China involve Chinese against Chinese companies, with only 20 percent of the cases involving disputes between Chinese and non-Chinese entities.

Worldwide Economic Recessions (Two of Them)

The world has gone through two major recessions in the past 10 years.

The first, the dot-com meltdown in 2001–2002 was focused primarily in Silicon Valley, which was the provider of Internet technology but had ripple effects around the United States for the millions of entrepreneurs who had invested their savings in websites, believing that their value would increase. While a few companies made fortunes (e.g., Microsoft), most start-ups—especially in the United States—were left without an exit strategy. In the resulting crash, many start-up companies failed, leaving behind only intangible assets. Those that had the foresight to protect and manage their assets—including patents—at least had an asset to potentially monetize. (See Case in Point: "Intellectual Ventures," further on in this chapter.) Today start-up CEOs are more aware of how patent assets are managed and what value they may potentially bring to the company.

The more recent economic crisis also taught CEOs a lesson about the importance of IP management, but the lesson was far more general. The main lesson of the 2008 financial crisis is that due to the multitude of risks that arise from business, regulatory, and human failings,[5] businesses must be alert to their true value. No matter how good a company's financial statements may look, its economic health is only as good as the cash flow its real assets and operations can generate—and the belief investors and lenders have in that value. Companies that manage their IP properly and send their IP message to their capital sources stand a better chance of surviving future recessions.

The Changing Legal Environment

The past decade has seen significant changes to the IP legal environment. In fact, the past 10 years have seen more IP cases in the Supreme

Court than the previous 50 years. These changes in IP law have led to an increase in complexity of IP cases. This in turn has helped to drive up the cost of IP litigation (approximately $5 million to try a case today compared with $2 million 10 years ago). IP litigation requires a great deal of capital. At the same time, damage awards have risen as well, so there can be a return on this investment. Furthermore, the rise of litigation funding means that the litigant need not always fund its own case; it can receive funding from a third-party investor, or utilize contingent-fee lawyers. All of this has made patent litigation a business unto itself—apart from invention and innovation. For a more detailed look at the significant IP cases over the past 10 years, please see Appendix A.

The Continuing Lack of a Formal IP Marketplace

As IP has increased in both strategic importance and value over the past two decades, the need for a stable marketplace has become ever more obvious. Looking back from the beginning of the second decade of the twenty-first century, it is clear that the IP community has not yet achieved this goal.

During the late 1990s a number of companies were formed, each offering its own version of an online marketplace for transacting intellectual property exchanges. For a variety of reasons, most of these companies no longer exist.

By the year 2000, IP monetization was still in its infancy—and generally limited to carrot-or-stick licensing. In a "carrot" license, a patent holder convinces a company to buy an attractive patent (carrot) on its own merits, so that the buyer can use it, or license it to others profitably. The alternative, "stick" license is offered to an actual or potential infringer: unless the prospect agrees to license, the patent holder will sue. Either way, when a company agrees to license a patent, payment is based on estimated future use over the life of the patent, plus past use when applicable.

Somehow, though, firms seeking customers for licensing or purchase of patents found it difficult to locate interested companies. Despite the promises implied by publications as our first Edison book, or another popular title of the same era, *Rembrandts in the Attic*, the emerging reality was that licensing of IP (whether as a carrot or as a stick) was difficult to accomplish, and outright sale of patents was largely limited to firms buying for litigation purposes or for risk reduction.

Case in Point: Intellectual Ventures

The financial dot-com "bubble" burst early in the new decade produced a spate of closures for technology start-ups. In 2003, former Microsoft members Nathan Myrvold and Edward Jung formed a company to acquire the IP assets from bankrupt organizations at firesale prices, and to provide operating companies with patent risk reduction. They formed Intellectual Ventures and began buying distressed patent assets as well as patent assets from individual investors who heretofore could find no market for their IP. Their initial buying criterion was simple; the patent assets must be valid but with infringement potential. Initially most of the assets were related to high technology; however, automotive, consumer products, and pharmaceutical patent assets were ultimately purchased.

Myrvold was able to attract over $5 billion in investment from both operating companies and institutional investors (primarily pension funds) to fuel his purchases. Once funded, Myrvold shifted his purchasing focus away from purely risk reduction for its operating company members, to buying valid and infringed patent assets across diverse technology areas whether or not a member participated in that area. This shift in focus did not go unnoticed in the IP community. Large operating companies quickly developed a concern that Myrvold and company were intent on asserting their patents against operating companies.

The effect of Myrvold's activity was to create a de facto market for patents. This attracted a number of firms to become brokers of patented assets. Brokers provided services to sellers by identifying the most attractive patents to sell, by performing the necessary (and costly) due diligence on the patents, and by locating buyers interested in the particular technology the patents protected.

The presence of several buyers and brokers suggested a business opportunity for someone to create a forum within which patent sales might take place. Ocean Tomo decided to offer such a service and in 2007 began a series of patent auctions, complete with auctioneer and gavel. The auctions packed the auction room with buyers, sellers, voyeurs, and their representatives.

Ocean Tomo conducted approximately seven auctions over a period of three years, and over that time several things became apparent. First, Intellectual Ventures and its intent to purchase were the driving engine of the auctions. Second, corporate sellers were generally offering their low-value patents for sale at auction. It also became clear that the old-fashioned auction approach had several limitations, not the least of which was the expense associated with putting it on, as well as the inconvenience to buyers and sellers for having to travel to the auction site and sacrifice two to three days of their valuable time.

By the fall of 2008 Intellectual Ventures stopped purchasing patents for its portfolio. When it ceased buying, the driving force behind the Ocean Tomo auctions evaporated. The auction, already under profitability pressures, was not able to sustain itself as a viable business, and subsequently sold its operations in 2009.

The Ocean Tomo experience crystallized several key factors associated with patent transactions:

- The cost of patent due diligence is very high.
- Until 2007 there was no standardization of seller packaging, which meant that each transaction was unique.
- There is little information and pricing transparency, which makes it difficult to determine what patents have been transacted and at what prices. This lack of transparency is a significant hindrance to the formation of an efficient and robust transaction market. Even with the lack of transparency issue, in 2008 the patent sale market was estimated to be over $1 billion a year.

The Rise of the IP Investor

Before 2001, the only investors interested in IP, and specifically patents, were those individuals about to lay out money for a large capital investment project such as a pharmaceutical drug development or the construction of a billion-dollar semiconductor lab. Other than that, investors thought IP was something to ask for, but not pay attention to. (Do you have any IP protection? If yes, check the box. If no, why not?) However, after the dot-com bust, many of the VCs found that IP was the only remaining asset left in the company—and the only way to get any return on their investment, which the VCs found was not always possible. Just because something is an asset does not mean that it will generate funds. IP, even if granted by the United States Patent and Trademark Office (USPTO) and carried on a company's books, is not always valid or valuable. Since recovering from the dot-com lessons, venture capitalists have paid more attention to IP. Mark Radcliffe, Senior Partner at DLA Piper in Palo Alto, explains:

> Venture capitalists have always fallen into two camps: (1) investors in life science companies and, (2) investors in IT companies. For the life sciences investor, intellectual property has always been a fundamental determinant for whether or not to make the investment. If you don't have a strong patent portfolio in the life science area, you don't have a company and no venture capitalist will invest. Patents for life science investors are so important that they break their rule of being reimbursed for all of their expenses: life science venture capitalists will pay a patent lawyer for a prior art search and an analysis of the patent portfolio of the perspective investment. So that's how unusual it is.
>
> On the IT side, while there is an increasing understanding of the importance of IP, investors are not as sophisticated as life science investors. However, in the last decade, IT venture capitalists have dramatically changed their view of patents. In the 1990s, IT venture capitalists did not ask about patents or a patent strategy. Now most VCs want to understand the patent strategy of a potential investment. One of my clients has filed over 200 patent applications, spending millions of dollars in legal fees, in

order to dominate a new market. This change in attitude has been driven in part by the increase in the period to an exit: the average period has lengthened from four or five years in the 1990s to eight years.

This longer period to exit provides sufficient time to prosecute patents and have them issued. However, I believe that the more important reason is that venture capitalists now understand that patents can be leveraged in an exit scenario to increase the price, because acquiring companies have become more interested in the patents of the startups that they are acquiring (in the last five years more than 80 percent of startups are acquired rather than going public).

An example of this behavior can be seen in Proteus Biomedical's funding presentation. As explained by Mark Zdeblick, CTO and cofounder of Proteus:

In the early years before we were funded, we spent a long time exploring different uses of silicon inside the body. We were specifically looking for implantable devices or electronics to add to existing therapies. There were two aspects to this. One was trying to figure out what types of electronics existing companies already had and landscaping that intersection with what people put inside the body and for what purpose. The other was a broad marketing role of trying to identify applications that would create significant value and then ultimately looking at white spaces where nobody had invented and creating art that was valuable, protectable, and would make a meaningful difference in people's lives.

We ended up focusing on the cardiac resynchronization therapy (CRT) business, betting that it was going to become a very important therapy for people with heart failure. We did not want to build our own pacemakers, CRT scans, and related infrastructure. Rather, we identified a partnering strategy from the very beginning: We would develop technology and license it to specifically Medtronic, St. Jude, and Guidant (which became Boston Scientific partway through our journey), and other smaller companies in the same vein of business. We had a focused partnering strategy and the only way to make such a partnering strategy work is to have intellectual property (IP) that is defensible and defining.

We used our IP in two different ways. One was to define the intellectual property landscape that we laid claim to and use it to distinguish and differentiate us from previous inventions in that area and the role that we'd play going forward and providing a therapy. It was essential to communicate this to our potential investors, first as a way of differentiating and also of defining what our business was going to be. To effectively maintain a partnering strategy, we had to show that our technology could influence the market share of one of these three players. If our technology could improve the response to therapy of an implant and shift market share towards our customer even a small amount, then a few dozen additional implants per year would pay for the asked investment in our company. This is based on a calculation of the increase in market capitalization resulting from each additional sale using the profit margins of each of those companies and their price-earnings multiples that existed at the time that we raised the money, about nine years ago.

Proteus was successful in their fund-raising efforts then and nine years later are still moving forward after multiple additional rounds of funding.

As VCs begin to see the importance of analyzing the IP of their prospective investments, other investors begin to notice IP as well. The dot-com bust, combined with the settlement paid as a result of *NTP vs. RIM*, helped ignite patent litigation as a business-model craze. Soon enterprising individuals were out seeking investment in IP litigation plays, such as Intellectual Ventures, ThinkFire, Rational Patent Exchange (RPX), Altitude Capital, and Round Rock, to name but a few. Intellectual Ventures, the most high profile of the lot, raised approximately $5 billion. While the jury is still out on whether it has in fact returned any significant cash value to its investors, it continues to exemplify the kind of optimism—and investment—that can accompany IP plays.

Summary

In this chapter we review some of the most significant highlights of the past 10 years and concede that so much has changed that it is time to incorporate more recent experiences and see how processes and theories regarding IP have evolved. Turn the page to find out how companies have adapted to this new world.

Chapter 3

Level One:
Defend Position

In the California Gold Rush days more than a century and a half ago, "forty-niners" learned that there was "gold in them thar' hills," but before breaking out a pan or pick axe, there were several things a miner had to do first. One of the most important of these was to stake and defend his claim. Today too, the first step in any venture is also defensive protection. This is the spirit of the Value Hierarchy's Level One: Defend Position.

Defense of intellectual property (IP)—including patents, trademarks, copyrights, and trade secrets as well as ownership offered through various types of agreements—is a necessary and desirable activity for a business. For example, patents, the most tangible form of intellectual property, give inventors adequate time to innovate (apply and market an idea) before others do.

Figure 3.1   Level One of the Value Hierarchy

Much as a miner must stake a claim in the land containing gold, or a shareholder must hold a stock certificate, a patent holder must file a patent. Only then can the owner of an invention begin to realize its desired value. But that is only the first step. To continue the Gold Rush metaphor, these steps might be seen as panning (Level Two, the initial savings of managing costs), mining (Level Three, deeper value capture), processing (Level Four, synthesizing opportunities), and, finally, sculpting into new forms (Level Five, shaping the future). These five levels constitute an overall process for the management of intellectual property—a process that depends on the foundation of *defense of ownership* (see Figure 3.1).

What Level One Companies Are Trying to Accomplish

We begin our discussion of best practices by focusing attention on the companies at the first level of IP Management: Defend Position. Firms operating at this level are concerned with the creation and management of sufficient numbers of patents to protect the firm's core intellectual property and to ensure defense against potential infringers. Companies at this level typically see the role of intellectual property as purely defensive.

The primary concerns for companies at this level are the classical defensive objectives:

- Protection of IP
- Avoidance of litigation
- Freedom to design

Companies at this level are often focused on accruing adequate depth and breadth of IP coverage to provide the desired protection. At Level One, companies are trying to accomplish four things:

1. Ensure that their business is adequately protected (creating and implementing processes for identifying intellectual property protection opportunities).
2. Create processes to facilitate patent generation and maintenance (screening these opportunities against the company's vision and strategy).
3. Create processes for enforcing patents (up to and including litigation).
4. Create educational programs regarding IP and its link to business value (emphasizing the theme of Level One, defense).

Activities for Level One companies focus on generating a sizable and relevant IP portfolio as quickly as possible. Companies at this level are concerned with the quantity and quality of IP output (effectiveness). While costs are a natural concern, they are usually of lesser importance than the need to obtain the desired protection; and protection is very important. Steve Fox, former Chief Intellectual Property Attorney at Hewlett-Packard, is fond of saying "One claim in one patent can put a company out of business!"

At Level One, companies are concerned with the portions of the IP Management System that are under the control of the IP attorneys (see Figure 3.2.)

IP attorneys at small Level One companies typically spend time with the creative and/or technical R&D people to learn what kind of new ideas or projects they are developing. Through these informal conversations, IP attorneys learn of ideas that are patentable, and then gather them into a prioritized list. In addition, they solicit "invention disclosures," informal, often one-page explanations of new ideas and their potential applications to the company's business or product lines. They give the highest ranking to ideas related to the company's key

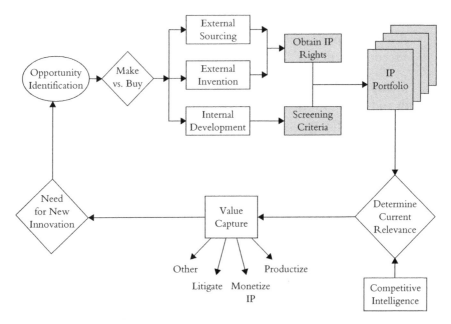

Figure 3.2 The IP Management System Showing Activities and Decisions Applicable to Level One

inventions, either technically (because the idea can improve the invention) or tactically (because the idea can leverage the invention). At large companies, attorneys tend to work with Business Unit leaders to learn about the kind of inventions the business wishes to obtain; they meet with groups of inventors to draw out new invention disclosures, sort and sift the disclosures, and categorize them according to their potential value to the firm.

This direct, dynamic approach to prioritizing and patenting the company's innovations has both advantages and disadvantages. On the advantage side, the method is simple, direct, inexpensive, and efficient—there is very little wasted effort. Nevertheless, there are some disadvantages that need to be mentioned. The process relies heavily on the IP attorney's ability to know what is valuable to the firm and its business units—including what is strategic, tactical, and/or marketable. Further, it assumes that IP attorneys are fully aware of competitors' business and patenting strategies, and can effectively use the company's patent creation process to neutralize competitor IP actions. Finally, the Level One approach assumes that attorneys are constantly apprised of any changes in company strategy and tactics so that they may revise the criteria used to screen inventions for patentability.

All of these expectations are worthy, but hardly realistic—especially in companies operating exclusively at Level One. Here intellectual property is used largely as a legal means to keep others out of their markets. Fortunately, thanks to the progress made in both the law and the courts, patents do indeed provide such protection. Not surprisingly, then, intellectual property in Level One companies is viewed almost entirely as a legal asset.

Functions, Tools, and Capabilities Quiz: Questions Only You Can Answer

Today, there are a number of software tools and service vendors to help companies visualize, analyze, and manage their intellectual property. In 2001 when *Edison* was first published, such tools and vendors were still relatively rare, but they have exploded in number since then. The current number and diversity of offerings make it difficult for managers to determine which might be the most useful for them, both for today and into the future. At Level One, IP managers primarily want a way to answer questions largely related to IP generation and its protection, and to increase IP awareness among managers. Since many tool providers claim that their product or service solves all corporate problems, Gathering companies at Level One have found it useful to review the list of questions following to prioritize their current and future needs, and to help determine what each tool provider can really deliver.

IP Portfolio Assessment
- Where is there overlap with competitors? With partners?
- What legal claims do our patents cover?
- How are invention disclosures reviewed and evaluated?
- Do we have current assignee information?
- Do we have the following information by technology categories:
  - What does it cost to prosecute and maintain our patents?
  - Where do we have gaps in the protection provided by our portfolio?
  - Can we group the portfolio by technology categories?

- What will it cost to prosecute and maintain each patent?
- What patents in the portfolio are related to current or future products?
- What patents have no relationship to either current of future products? Are any of those potentially valuable to someone else?
- What is the return on investment (ROI) of each patent?
- How does the portfolio relate to business strategy/priorities? Are we "overinvented"?
- In what areas are there portfolio gaps versus strategy, versus markets, or versus competitors? What are we missing? What are the "white spaces"?
- How valuable/strong are my patents compared to my competitors' patents?
- How is my portfolio evolving? How are my competitor's portfolios evolving?

Docketing

- How can we effectively manage our prosecution and maintenance process?
- How do we handle trade secrets?
- How do we track ideas from invention disclosure to filing status?
- What needs to be filed and paid . . . when and where?
- What should our budget for patent prosecution and maintenance be?
- Robust budget and cost forecast model.
- Real-time reporting of financial information.

Patent Quality

- Are the patents valid?
- How broad are the claims?
- Have we ensured design freedom?
- How enforceable are the patents?

Searching

- Can you determine the following?
  - Validity.
  - Right to practice.
  - Where are the patents enforceable?

○ Relevance mapping not citation-based.
○ What patents are available and at what prices?
○ Monitoring of litigation.
○ Finding foreign counterparts easily.
○ Prosecution history.
○ Removal of duplicates.
○ Where are the "white spaces"?
○ Should we continue to invest in a technology?
○ Does prior art knock it out?
○ Impacts of court rulings on each patent.

Litigation

- What has been published relevant to the specific subject area?
- What products might infringe specific claims?
- What can I counterassert?
- What is our access to court filings (motions, etc.)?
- How does the data support (or not support) each claim?
- What is my company's appetite for litigation?
- What are potential litigation alerts?
- By company and by technology, what are the past judgments and what are the pending cases?

Patent Value

- What are the number of claims and number of independent claims?
- Does the value change by geography or by industry segment?
- How is the patent being used in existing products and services?
- For what amount should we sell the portfolio?
- Link value to financials. Value of each patent. Internal transfer pricing value.
- Likely infringement penalty costs (past use) and likely royalty cost (future use).
- How is the patent being used in offered products and services?
- Tables of betas by SIC code.
- Royalty rate database.
- Patent quality (validity and scope).
- Market impact of each patent.

Competitive Assessment

- Who are competitors' key inventors?
- What are the technology trends?
- Where are the "white spaces"?
- Comparison of multiple portfolios.
- What is the level of patenting activity by company and by technology? Its size and shape?
- Where is innovation happening along the value chain?
- Ongoing monitoring for potential infringement.
- How do my competitors' patents compare with mine?
- Identify potential collaboration partners.
- Who owns the most commonly cited prior art?

The Federal Circuit

Defense is integral to IP management in any company. Fortunately, staking a claim in intellectual assets is easier today than ever before, especially where patents are concerned. Patent appeals are now centralized in one court: the U.S. Court of Appeals for the Federal Circuit, known as the "Federal Circuit,"[*] which has exclusive jurisdiction over all patent appeals from other federal courts.

When viewed in light of nearly 200 years of patent law evolution, the Federal Circuit court is relatively new. It was created with the merger of the U.S. Court of Claims and the U.S. Court of Customs and Patent Appeals—a consolidation ordered as part of the Federal Courts Improvements Act of 1982.[†] The courts certainly needed improvement from a patent law perspective. Before 1982, it was not only ineffective to defend a patent by suing over infringement; it was plain risky. In the so-called Black-Douglas era (named for the Supreme Court Justices Hugo Black and William O. Douglas), the courts feared the monopoly potential of patents and discouraged them accordingly. In this era, the chances of a

[*]This court is one of 13 federal circuit courts of appeal. (The other dozen serve the 12 main legal regions in the United States.)
[†]Federal Courts Improvement Act of 1982, Pub. L. No. 97–164, 96 Stat. 25 (1982).

patent being held valid and enforced against infringement were merely one in three.

The U.S. courts, rather than focusing on the wrongdoing of the infringer, tended to focus on the protectability of the allegedly infringed patent, and often declared patents invalid. Consider the classic case of Westinghouse. Long before its restructuring and merger into CBS and later Viacom, the electronics giant sought to protect its circuit breaker patents. In 1979, it petitioned the International Trade Commission to block Hitachi's circuit breaker imports on the grounds that Hitachi was infringing one of Westinghouse's patents. The federal courts ruled that the Westinghouse patent was not valid.[*] Westinghouse's attempt to defend its own rights caused those rights to be taken away.

This sad era in patent law is now long gone. The Federal Circuit of today is handing down decisions more favorable to patent holders, making defense worthwhile. The protectability of intellectual ideas is a new and valuable notion, says Mark Radcliffe, a Senior Partner with DLA Piper LLC:

> It has only been in the last 20 years that intellectual property and especially patents were regarded in U.S. courts, not as the tools of monopolists, but as critical to national economic well-being. Furthermore, it is now generally accepted that such innovation cannot occur unless companies that succeed in the marketplace can recoup their research, development, and marketing costs. The upshot is that intellectual property is now viewed as playing a key role in developing technologies for the next century.

[*]Hisamitsu Arai, "The Facts behind Japan's Technology Explosion," *Managing Intellectual Property* (May 2000), 19ff.

Virtually all companies owning intellectual property, and patents in particular, are likely to find that adherence to the principles, processes, and best practices identified in this chapter will be of significant benefit.

Best Practices for Level One: Defend Position

What, then, is the best way to defend IP assets? The current practice of defending one's position is adequate, but not ideal. Having a narrow, permanent defensive mentality can cause companies to incur unnecessary costs and forsake potential commercial opportunities for capturing value. To be an "Edison" company requires a pragmatic approach—one that adopts certain best practices.

So, let's look at the practical application of defensive IP management, and examine some of the best practices used by other defenders.

In our own work, as well as with the experiences of Gathering companies, we have been able to define four best practices areas that companies excelling at enlightened defense incorporate into their IP management function. They are:

Best Practice 1: Taking Stock of What You Own
Best Practice 2: Obtaining and Maintaining IP
Best Practice 3: Building IP Awareness
Best Practice 4: Enforcing Defensively

Best Practice 1: Taking Stock of What You Own

The value of research and development (R&D) is often invisible—not only to outsiders, but to IP managers as well. That great new technology just perfected by your R&D department and patented by your legal group will never appear as an asset on your company's balance sheet because it was internally generated, rather than purchased from someone else. Will you remember that it is there?

In our consulting practices it is not unusual for us to interview corporate officers and find that they have no idea how many patents their companies have in their portfolios. Even with the few who do, it is often the case that they have no real understanding of those inventions—what they are and what broader commercial purpose they serve. This is not surprising. Prior to introduction of recent computer software programs designed to help manage intellectual property, the only way for managers to know what was in their patent portfolios was to read each individual patent.

Companies are now able to download the contents of their patent portfolios from a variety of online sources. If nothing else, companies should create a list of all of their intellectual property that has been granted, filed, and is currently pending.

According to Sezmi's Erik Oliver, "The first step in getting a handle on your intellectual property is to know what you own. Companies need to inventory their intellectual property that has been granted, filed, and is currently in process and update it routinely." An intangibles audit list includes the following:

- All inventions that are not the subject of issued patents, but may be the subject of patent applications, or where the company may be able to establish dates for invention, discovery, or reduction to practice dates.
- All software developed by or for the company.
- All known trade secrets from which the company derives economic benefit by keeping it secret.
- Documents reflecting the company's policies and procedures relating to the creation, maintenance, and protection of trade secrets, such as the company's written confidentiality policies and nondisclosure agreements.
- Documents relating to hiring and exit interviews of technology and other sensitive personnel.
- Any agreements with third parties pertaining to intellectual property, including nondisclosure agreements (often called NDAs), noncompete agreements, joint venture agreements, and any partnerships related to the exchange of intellectual property.
- Any documentation relating to proprietary know-how, such as a description and the place or person in whom it resides.
- All license agreements, whether the company is the licensor or licensee.

The subject of licenses merits additional explanation. A *license* is the direct granting of permission by a governing entity to a governed entity—as when a local government permits a business to operate within its jurisdiction. A *license agreement* is an agreement between two parties (companies and/or individuals) regarding the use of intellectual property. License agreements can be for an *in-license* or an *out-license*. An in-license agreement enables a company to use, adapt, sell, or otherwise benefit from another company's invention (by keeping the revenues from the invention but paying the inventor for its use). An out-license does the converse, enabling a company with an invention to get that invention to market with the help of another company (by authorizing another company to use the technology in exchange for a license fee). The inventory of licensing agreements in a company with a large and diverse IP portfolio should generally include both "in" and "out" licenses. Some companies engage in numerous cross-licenses—discussed further below.

Licenses are essential to the ability of a corporation to continue to conduct its business. Therefore, the IP function should ensure that all such necessary licenses are current and in good order. To use licenses effectively, a company should review the proper documents pertaining to licenses, including:

- All intellectual property licenses where the company is *licensor* (via an in-license), including names of parties, dates of expiration, rights granted, and any pertinent restrictions.
- All intellectual property licenses where the company is a *licensee* (via an out-license), including names of parties, dates of expiration, rights granted, and any pertinent restrictions such as territory or transferability.

There are degrees of taking stock of the IP you own. At its most basic, this might involve creating a simple Excel spread sheet that lists each patent or other item in column A and then other pertinent information about the item in subsequent columns. For a patent, this would include date of issue, date the patent expires, dates and amounts for country patent maintenance fees, and so forth.

At a more ambitious level, taking stock of what you own might involve a more in-depth analysis of each patent to supplement the foregoing simple information. For example, each patent might be tagged by its technology, and by the business unit it supports. It might also be identified with the kind of value the company seeks to obtain from this patent, as well as its intended use. For Cargill, an initial intellectual property inventory completely changed the company's IPM practices from trying to keep everything as a secret, to putting in place more layered protection. Harry Gwinnell, Vice President and Chief Intellectual Property Counsel for Cargill, recounts his story on the importance of inventorying your IP:

> At Cargill our CEO often comments that it is important for Cargill to know what it is that Cargill knows. This clearly applies to IP as well. You have to know what IP you have in order to take advantage of and to extract value from it. I was Cargill's first Chief Intellectual Property Counsel. Up to that time, the company had managed its proprietary information almost exclusively by calling them "trade secrets," but no one really knew the identity of all of these so-called trade secrets, nor were there any effective companywide practices in place to maintain them as secret. One of my early initiatives was to really push for patenting some of the company's innovative ideas and, even more importantly, to create a database of all of the company's IP: patents, trademarks, trade secrets, and the IP agreements that were associated with particular products and services. You can imagine what a competitive advantage this has provided for us over the years since its inception.

Whether your inventory turns up only a few patents or many, it is wise to encourage the creation of more patents. This means, in part, encouraging invention—an important aspect of patent acquisition. (In addition, patents can be acquired from other companies, but this is not always possible or optimal.) This leads to Best Practice 2.

Best Practice 2: Obtaining and Maintaining IP

Obtaining granted patents is not the end objective of patent management, but rather the beginning. Once a patent is in the portfolio it provides a number of new challenges for the portfolio manager. These include regular reviews of the business value of the patent to the firm, routine payments of patent maintenance fees, security of the information in the portfolio, and ensuring that the coverage provided by the portfolio's contents is adequate to support the company's business strategies and objectives.

Elisabeth Sussex, Director of Intellectual Property for Proteus Biomedical, discusses this best practice area from her perspective:

When a company is in start-up mode, its IP process involves three sets of activities: ideating, creating, and protecting selected inventions with IP. In our early stage, patenting was a reflection of the organization at that time: business development, technical and scientific, and the IP group. These three groups worked as individual, isolated islands of expertise, occasionally bumping into one another, and the bumping sometimes produced a patent application. I joined Proteus Biomedical shortly after it transitioned out of its start-up phase.

Fortunately, the company recognized how productive it would be to coalesce the workings of the three groups and to develop better integrative links between them. Three critical and complementary innovative processes took place at about the same time.

First, the IP department took a step back, and decided to rethink the processes involved with obtaining and managing the company's patents. It began by clearly understanding the company's business goals. We met with all of the company's business and engineering people and developed a clear and mutually agreed-upon understanding of the company's business goals.

From that beginning, we were able to map a set of IP goals and an IP strategy that supported the business goals of the company. From this exercise, a new patenting process emerged, one that departed from the one used during the company's start-up phase, and one that was more focused on patents as both defensive and commercial assets.

The second innovative process involved our technology sector. The company formed an Advanced Technology Group, which placed a greater emphasis on identifying technology trends and evaluating innovation versus invention.

The third innovative process involved the business development folks, who stepped back and began to focus on identifying new and interesting markets and products for Proteus to consider.

Several good things came out of the convergence of the three foregoing efforts. Most important, the IP department began to get involved in the development process at a much earlier point in time, which allowed us to bring information about the IP landscape to the business and engineering people early in the game. Also, with each of the three groups providing critical and complementary information at the outset of an endeavor, the fused information allowed us to go forward faster and with a greater degree of assurance of good outcomes than had been the case earlier when the company was using the start-up mode approach.

But patents are only one form of intellectual property receiving attention at leading companies. Mark Connolly, the IP Director for Central R&D, Industrial Biosciences & Patent Searching at DuPont, a company with a long history of obtaining and managing all forms of intellectual property, explains what his company is doing to protect trade secrets:

> DuPont has always been diligent about protecting our IP through patents or by maintaining trade secrets; whichever route provided better protection. We have a "cradle to grave" approach that considers the IP risks most closely associated with the technology development pipeline, from new concepts through product development, and puts managing processes in place to mitigate these risks (see Figure 3.3).
>
> In 2005, we identified a major internal theft of proprietary information that forced us to rethink current practices and take our trade secret protection processes to a higher level. We found the employee thief because we had just installed a new electronic document management system—called Electronic Data Library (EDL)—where technical progress reports and other critical information are stored. We observed that a particular employee accessed 15 times as many documents as the second most active user in DuPont. If it wasn't for the information associate who saw the usage blip, we might not have caught the guilty party. We found out that he had downloaded over 22,000 scientific abstracts and 16,000 full text documents— that's something. (Downloading this amount of information was difficult back in 2005 when the maximum hard-drive capacity was about 200 megabytes.)[1]
>
> At the time, employee theft was not on our radar screen. Like many companies, we thought all of our employees were good

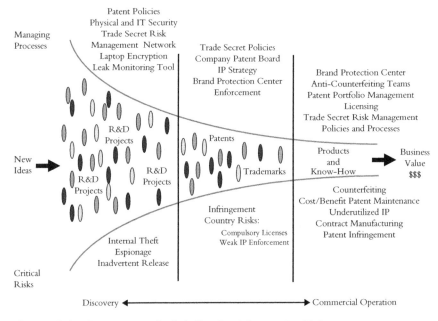

Figure 3.3   Responses to Intellectual Property Risks

people. It never occurred to us that a theft such as this could happen, that an "insider" would deliberately steal massive amounts of documents with the intent to sell or otherwise transmit them to our competitors. At that point we asked ourselves, "What do we do to prevent this from happening again?"

The first thing we did was to inform and educate the company's senior leaders about the incident, and asked them to reinforce the importance of protecting proprietary information within the organizations. We wanted strong top-down communications. We also wanted the leaders to understand that this could happen to them and might cause serious harm to their businesses.

The R&D, Legal, Security, and IT communities then got together to develop improved high-level corporate policies and procedures, developing a multi-year plan to substantially improve the way DuPont protects its know-how. Part of the plan was to more clearly differentiate between intangible assets that were protected (patents, trademarks, and notebooks) and trade secrets or know-how that was sitting unprotected.

In research, by definition, almost everything is a trade secret. So how does a company balance its needs to protect its secrets on the one hand with its desire to encourage and to nurture an innovative, open and collaborative work environment on the other? The two appear to be in conflict.

In the past, when we lived in a paper world, DuPont had an annual campaign where everyone audited themselves to ensure that all paper documents complied with our records retention criteria. For example, whereas notebooks are classified as "Keep Forever," other documents might be classified with a retention period of three years. Furthermore, all documents were classified as "confidential to DuPont," not confidential but for "internal use only" or "public domain."

A final category, applied to a very select few documents, was called "confidential special control." These comprised trade secrets whose loss would cause irreparable harm to DuPont. When the company was still in paper mode, it was relatively easy to identify our documents, classify them accordingly, and keep our confidential information under lock and key.

Now that we are in the digital information age, it is possible for each employee to save more than 100 gigabytes of data on their laptops. Our trade secret protection program reinforces the continuing need to classify all documents—electronic and paper—according to the categories that were developed years ago and reminds our employees that there really are different degrees of trade secrets.

We found that we had to do a lot of additional training to describe the sensitivity categories and how electronic information within each category was to be handled. For example, what does it really mean for information to be classified as confidential or confidential special control? It means that the information involves our most critical trade secrets. The information might be related to the plant design, technical standards, and operating procedures for the process to manufacture DuPont Kevlar fiber. It might be the customer lists and margins for DuPont Tyvek business.

In the research environment, we began by educating our scientists. We described in great detail the types of technical trade secrets that exist, something that hadn't been clearly articulated before. Then the R&D units developed a complete inventory, business by business, of what they saw as our most critical secrets. They could be most critical because they have to do with a government project and cannot be disclosed. They may be most critical because they're cutting-edge technology that could form an entirely new business and patent applications had not been filed. If divulged outside the company, this information could enable others to enter the business more quickly and with less R&D investment, and could preclude DuPont from obtaining patent protection.

Once we had identified the information that was most critical to DuPont, our next step was to put rigorous procedures in place to restrict access to the critical information on a need-to-know basis. Owners of electronic information, like online team rooms, are required to update and review the access control list on a quarterly basis. We now have layers of security to protect our most critical trade secrets (the rule of thumb is that you want four layers of security). Physically getting into the site is the first layer, getting into the building is the second, getting into the office is the third, and finally having access to the computer or file cabinets is the fourth. We tried to carefully think through the issues associated with physical security as well as electronic security.

More recently, we started an additional process to enhance the security of our everyday electronic documents called digital rights management. This process allows an information owner to take individual documents and share them with others in a secure and well documented way. For each document, the owner identifies the people who can access the information, and gives them rights to view, print, and/or read the document. Further, the document can be given a "self-destruct" date after which it is unreadable. We can now take our most critical documents and lock them down in a way that only people with a need to know have access and we can easily track when the documents are opened and by whom. We have also begun to deploy (as law permits) software that logs and controls data file movement in and out of each computer. When a file is written to any external media (USB, CD drive) from a computer, the software records it to a central database. When a document is e-mailed outside of DuPont to your AOL account, the transaction is recorded. Business and functional units are allowed to set a default level of control, then customize it for individual groups as necessary. As an example, this control can warn us if documents are accessed from certain repositories or servers and moved to external media or e-mailed, or prevent it altogether.

We've tried to raise awareness of the need to protect our trade secrets to a level rivaling that of our core values: safety, health and environmental protection, respect for people, and the conduction of business with the highest ethical behavior. Protecting our know-how needs to be yet another value central to the way we do our jobs. At the individual employee level, it's about protecting our company's secrets, keeping our products profitable, developing new products faster and better than our competition, and ultimately saving our jobs. That's what trade secret protection is all about.

Best Practice 3: Building IP Awareness

One of the difficulties faced by IP managers is the need to educate executives and employees alike about IP in a meaningful way. Managers must explain to all hands why IP is important to their firm and what they need to do to develop and protect it.

Here, Gene Potkay, Senior Vice President of Intellectual Property at Nielsen, describes his experience with raising awareness about IP in this well-known market research and ratings firm:

Nielsen's business involves measuring the media that people watch on television and online, and what people buy, both online and in brick-and-mortar stores. Enabling that kind of measurement requires the creative use of a lot of technology, giving us the capability to collect, aggregate, and then analyze large amounts of data with a good deal of analytics, statistics, and modeling while ensuring individual consumer privacy at the same time.

My arrival at Nielsen supported an earlier decision the company had made to invigorate and build upon its nascent focus on managing its IP. My earliest task was to develop a plan for doing that.

The first step was to assess the current state of affairs and to understand what was currently happening. It seemed to me that we needed to understand both the company's IP management capabilities and the expectations of our internal customers—their level of understanding of IP and its capability to support their business—before it made sense to set about making any improvements. What was working, what was broken, and what simply didn't exist?

We learned that the current IP management function was a small operation with internal processes and practices that were ad-hoc and not scalable. We also learned that there were several key managers who were believers in intellectual property and the kinds of value it could provide for their businesses, while others were less convinced.

It became apparent that there were two general efforts that needed to pursue. The first was to reinvigorate the methods and practices for generating and managing the firm's intellectual property; the second was to build a broad base of awareness and understanding of why IP is important to the firm and what it could do to improve Nielsen's competitive position.

Next up, Gary Bender, Head of Global Intellectual Property at Visa, describes his experience in building awareness:

> I arrived at Visa in 2008 immediately following its IPO. My job is to take the intellectual property of the newly combined global entity at Visa and make it a coordinated program commensurate with the needs of the company, and the opportunities afforded the company by growth and new products.
>
> Initially, I spent a great amount of time throughout the global organization educating thousands of people on the fundamentals of intellectual property and what it offers to each of our businesses. Also, I would talk about the opportunities and risks associated with IP and its management. On the opportunity side I would speak about how much technology, know-how,

and intellectual horsepower Visa possesses, demonstrating with examples and what the company has built so far and what we are building currently.

As it turned out, the timing was perfect. The company had just gone public and had changed from an organization owned and managed by its member banks to one that was its own independent entity. That meant that although the fundamentals of our business and our strategy were largely unchanged, the way in which we structured ourselves had changed dramatically, so everyone was open to new ideas and ways of going about things.

Scott Frank, President and CEO of AT&T Intellectual Property, offers another perspective. He describes AT&T's approach to IP awareness:

At AT&T we have noticed that our employees are naturally grouped into three sets, based on their use and impact of the company's intellectual property. For example, about 1 percent of the people in the company are high-IP-propensity employees. These are the employees with whom the IP organization spends a lot of time. This set includes people like the CTO, CSO, CIO and President of the labs and key technical people on their teams. Another key group of high-IP-propensity employees are those who negotiate technology development contracts, such as the Chief Procurement Officer and key front line negotiators on his or her team. The high-IP-propensity set also usually includes the CMO, Corporate Brand Officer and key brand managers on their teams. We all need to be in sync on IP projects we're working on and the strategies we will utilize.

The second tier, let's say the next nine percent of employees, represents the people who need to have a working knowledge of IP. They know who comprises the IP team and who they can contact when they have some kind of business matter involving IP.

The other 90 percent are people with whom my team rarely or never speaks directly, but who need to be aware of the importance of IP to the company and what their responsibilities about it may be. For this group of employees, the IP team needs to mount awareness campaigns, typically through special events, internal publications, and e-mails. This will, at the very least, get them socialized about IP and to enable them to handle some of the IP basics on their own.

Best Practice 4: Enforcing Defensively

Our final Level One best practice concerns enforcement. Level One best practices focus on using IP as a legal asset, and therefore when we speak of enforcement we are speaking of it as a defensive measure. We will discuss litigation as a monetization tool in later chapters of this book. In our consulting practice, we routinely hear from executives that they are reluctant to enforce their patents based upon the ever-increasing cost of patent litigation, and the public relations downside of looking too aggressive.

According to a widely cited report from the American Intellectual Property Law Association, as of 2010 the cost of median patent litigation is \$5.5 million.[2] The question we pose to these executives is, "Why spend any money on intellectual property if you are not willing to enforce defensively the rights you have?" What do we mean by "enforce defensively"? We are speaking about enforcing your IP for any of the following purposes:

- To send a message: Many companies litigate selectively to ensure that they create a reputation for their willingness to enforce. Microsoft is a good example of a firm that has a reputation (with lawsuits to back it up) of a willingness to enforce against both large and small companies.
- To gain market advantage: To keep competitors and/or infringers out of your market, and to increase their cost of goods sold through licensing and thereby give you a significant cost advantage.

Summary

Defense is necessary and desirable. Indeed, as a basis for future activities, defense can be a valuable way to gain IP territory for future development. And there are times for any company when the majority of attention and energy must be devoted to defense. But companies should not get "stuck" at Level One, refusing to operate outside it.

Instead, they should use defense pragmatically, as one of many IP-related activities.

The four best practices in defense described in this chapter—taking stock of what you own, obtaining and maintaining patents, building IP awareness, patents, and enforcing your patents defensively—can all help a company stake a claim in its own future.

Claim staking is a wise move for all kinds of companies—not only technology-oriented companies. True, intangibles-rich companies are more successful in the current environment, as noted in our Introduction. But this is partly because the managers of these companies spend the necessary time and energy creating or acquiring those intangibles, and then *claiming and protecting* them in order to develop them.

Any company can do this! Returning to our metaphor of the California Gold Rush, it is useful to note that James Marshall, the man credited with discovering gold in California, spotted it while on the job at Sutter's Mill, a humble sawmill. He recognized the value of the glint of gold in the stream, and immediately reported it to his employer. The rest is history.

In a similar vein, the "sawmills" of today need to be on the lookout for intellectual property. We will see this more clearly in the next four chapters as we move beyond Level One defensive activities to review activities in the other levels: Level Two: Manage Cost; Level Three: Capture Value; Level Four: Synthesize Opportunities; and Level Five: Shape the Future.

Yes, even sawmill businesses and similar "old economy" businesses have assets that require protection. The CEO of a forest products company once lamented the lack of intellectual capital in his industry. He defined intellectual capital as some form of sophisticated technology. In an effort to impress us with his company's attempts to fill this IC void, he told us that his firm had recently purchased and installed some sophisticated computer-controlled machinery for milling logs, but that it had been unable to produce the same amount of usable lumber per log as the company's human sawmill operators. When we pointed out to him that the mill hands and their knowledge and know-how were the very essence of intellectual capital for his firm, he looked surprised, and then acknowledged that he had never considered intellectual capital in that way.

As in the Gold Rush, the most important step is protection—the staking of a claim. So before putting all of your assets into your own Gold Rush, make sure that your company has staked its proper claims. Like Thomas Edison, keep your eyes open for hidden value, and then secure ownership of that value for a more prosperous future. To build that prosperous future, continue on the journey toward the boardroom, moving on to the next level, Managing Costs.

Chapter 4

Level Two: Manage Costs

Level Two is the second level of intellectual property (IP) management evolution for firms involved with IP (see Figure 4.1). Companies at Level Two are in defensive mode, just as they were at Level One. The difference is that Level Two companies have realized that IP, particularly patents, can be both expensive and lucrative, so they want to increase the returns on the dollars they invest. Indeed, companies at this level have come to realize that IP is a business investment, one that requires keen management attention and astute cost-benefit analysis. For this reason, companies at Level Two find themselves interested in activities that reduce cost, increase efficiency, increase effectiveness, and raise productivity.

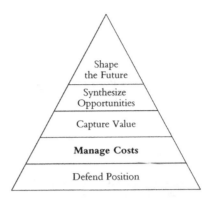

Figure 4.1   Level Two of the Value Hierarchy

What Level Two Companies Are Trying to Accomplish

Companies at Level Two take a somewhat broader view of defensive activity than do companies at Level One. Although both use similar elements in their IP management decision systems, Level Two companies are trying to accomplish four things:

1. Relate the portfolio to the organization's business.
2. Establish a screening criterion.
3. Manage IP costs.
4. Begin to consider "make versus buy" technology and IP decisions.

At the same time that Level Two companies are working toward these goals, they are also engaged in two creative processes: (1) generating patents and (2) refining the processes they use to manage them.

At Level Two, patent portfolios and patenting processes are already in place. Management efforts in Level Two are directed at improving the patenting and patent management processes to minimize costs and to maximize the defensible benefits from patents.

In the previous chapter, we did not mention the management of costs, and for a good reason. Companies operating primarily at the "Defend Position" (Level One in our pyramid) often lack formal cost-control measures. They tend to review patents on an individual basis and are often blind to aggregate costs.

By contrast, companies operating at the "Manage Costs" level take a more comprehensive view of their patent portfolio. They are able to see the patterns and can aggregate all of the costs associated with IP and its management. They separate small-dollar decisions from large-dollar ones—dealing with the former routinely, while giving an extra level of review to the latter.

The benefits of such scrutiny are obvious. By reducing costs, companies increase their profits. This is particularly true in the later years of the life cycle of patents, when costs become higher.

In our consulting practices, it is not unusual to find that anywhere from 20 percent to 50 percent of a company's portfolio is no longer useful and could be eliminated. Thus, just by reviewing their portfolio, many firms could realize immediate savings of hundreds of thousands of dollars! This chapter describes how and where companies should look to better manage their costs.

Companies operating at the "Manage Costs" level are much more proactive about patents than are companies operating at the "Defend Position" level. For Level Two companies it is important to inventory the patents currently in the company's portfolio as well as the patent applications the company is prosecuting. New software packages have greatly enhanced this previously tedious process. For example, many vendors offer special software that can automate docketing—the tracking of the patenting management process from filing to expiration.

The electronic IP inventory systems used by sophisticated Level Two companies are more functional than simple reminder systems. They help companies better understand how to link their innovations to cash flow, by allowing routine, easy access to information that shows whether a patent is worth maintaining or should be permitted to lapse. Some companies have even gone so far as to create their own internal applications, although most find it easier to purchase and adapt commercially available software to meet their unique needs.

Level Two companies also make it a point to get information about what competitors are doing—a process made easier in recent years due to changes in the law. Until November 2000, patents remained confidential during the filing phase and were published only at the time they were issued, or sometimes years later (2 to 10 was the average time frame). The law has changed such that, except under certain circumstances, all patent applications are now published 18 months after filing. To find out what patents have been issued and what patent applications have been published by the U.S. Patent and Trademark Office, for example, one merely needs to look up the agency's website: www.uspto.gov.

Companies at Level Two have learned that there is a business logic that can define the kind of intellectual property their firm requires. Further, they are beginning to understand that each kind of intellectual property (whether patent, trademark, copyright, or trade secret) protects very specific forms of expression or concept and, in addition, can provide very specific value related to the company's business activities.

At Level Two, the person overseeing the company's IP portfolios is concerned with more than just the legal aspects of IP management. He or she must be involved with how IP is to be used in the business and also in the "make versus buy" decision as well as with all of the processes associated with obtaining protected innovations.

Therefore, Level Two companies are exploring the IP management system activities that can make it more efficient and effective to obtain new patents for their portfolio (see Figure 4.2).

Best Practices for Level Two: Manage Costs

Commercially available tools and services are valuable as far as they go, but Level Two companies go further. They adopt a series of best practices, often including these four:

Best Practice 1: Relate the portfolio to business use.
Best Practice 2: Create a screening criterion.
Best Practice 3: Manage the patent portfolio in a cost-conscious manner.
Best Practice 4: Begin discussions regarding "make versus buy" innovation preferences.

Best Practice 1: Relate the Portfolio to Business Use

Fundamental to the intent of companies at Level Two is the need to increase the efficiency and effectiveness of their patenting activities. In

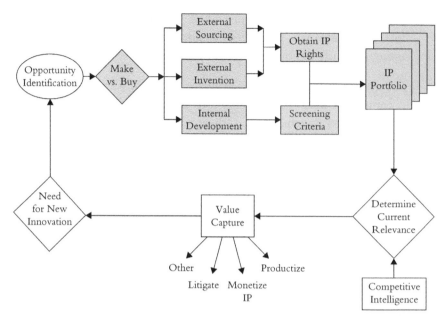

Figure 4.2 The IPMS Showing Activities and Decisions Applicable to Level Two

accomplishing this goal, companies must be able to match patents with the firm's business strategies and objectives. Specifically, they will want to categorize current and prospective patents and innovations in ways that facilitate both tactical and strategic decisions about these capabilities. Any system or framework that enables this process will be valued at a Level Two firm.

To more effectively manage their intellectual property portfolios, it is important for companies to first know what their portfolios contain. This involves knowing not only simple portfolio demographics (e.g., number of patents and technologies, technology groupings, remaining patent life, etc.), but also information about the content or usability of the patents. Such information is useful for three reasons:

1. To obtain a clear picture of corporate technology assets and their value to support further strategic decisions and transactions.
2. To be able to capitalize on technologies and their value as they become less valuable for internal use (usually due to changes in corporate strategy or market acceptance).

3. To have a capability for providing information to stakeholders (investors, customers, employees, vendors, etc.) on the state of development and use of company technology assets.

There is no single best way to evaluate a company's patent portfolio. Some companies may make a conscious decision to keep only patents related to their core technology. Others may obtain patents that do not relate to their core technology, but can protect against competition. In some firms following this practice, as few as 3 percent of patents may be used to support current business. Is this practice good or bad? The answer depends on the nature of the company's industry and the nature of the invention being patented. What is important is to establish a classification scheme for the portfolio.

Companies categorize their intellectual property portfolios differently. Some companies classify the portfolio based on technology areas through International Patent Classification (IPC) codes, for example. Other companies classify their portfolio by business division. And yet others categorize their portfolio as "must have," "nice to have," and "junk (not currently used by this company)." When one company reviewed its "must have" category, 30 percent were "nice to have" and 50 percent were "junk." Today, by following the best practices described for Levels One and Two in this book, that company has a different profile. It has more than doubled its percentage of "must have" patents to 45 percent, and it maintains few if any "junk" patents.

Steve Baggott, Director of Global Business Development at Procter & Gamble, reviews the evolution of his company's journey toward a best practice in this area:

> Patent attorneys have traditionally been very influential in making business decisions where IP is involved. In the early years, the company looked to its patent attorneys to determine what they saw as the most important things for R&D to work on—and what they wouldn't. They worked closely with the R&D teams to understand the technology and potential benefit, but the link to business strategy was not as strong as it is today. As a result, we weren't always working on the projects that might matter most. We were missing an effective connection

between three key areas for our business—legal, R&D, and the business leaders.

As we moved into the 1990s, P&G began to take a much more intentional and concerted strategic view for how we manage our intellectual property for our own internal commercialization. This meant that the IP attorneys were given a seat at the business table. They became fully exposed to (and contributed to) determining what the business choices were. So, fast-forward to today, and look at any P&G business unit that operates on a global basis, you will see that it assembles the business leadership team routinely to review business results as well as to review initiative programs. The IP attorneys have a very important role to play in those discussions.

This describes how P&G's IP management function has grown, strengthened, and become an even more effective and strategic part of our company's operations over the last two decades. In fact, this growth in the importance of the IP function at P&G has been part of enabling what we've been able to do in Global Business Development because what we do is so closely linked to the company's IP.

Gene Potkay, Senior Vice President Intellectual Property at Nielsen, was hired by the company to re-energize an IP management activity that the company hadn't previously considered particularly strategic. He explains:

Early on I tested the waters in my new company by making a few presentations to our business units proposing a few different alternative options to leverage IP to support their businesses. I came away with the feeling that I had thrown ice water on the party. Up until that point, Nielsen's dominant mind-set about intellectual property was primarily a singular, tactical and defensive one: patents are created for, and are only good for, immediate assertion against infringing entities.

In contrast, senior management and I had decided that the company first needed to build a foundation of solid patents in the portfolio for overall defensive purposes. Once that was achieved, the company could then devote more attention to policing infringements, monetizing our portfolio, and finding other more novel ways to leverage the company's IP assets.

I obtained agreement at the topmost level for the company's near-term IP strategy and provided the executives at the top with a number of options at a high level about why it is important to patent, and left it at that. Thereafter, we set out to get buy-in at the grassroots levels of our business units. Our first challenge was to invigorate the portfolio with new patents that met the company's strategic business objectives.

It was apparent that we needed to increase the flow of new ideas and inventions by retooling and energizing the company's invention disclosure process. We established a reward and recognition program to generate higher quality invention disclosures in substantially greater numbers directed to patentable ideas much more focused on our commercially important business objectives. The new program rewards inventors at three stages: on submittal of an invention disclosure, on company submittal of a first-filed patent application, and on granting of a U.S. patent. For invention disclosures, the program provides a modest reward for submission of well-thought-out and articulated invention disclosures. These awards are often gift certificates that can be redeemed from an online catalog. Every quarter, we afford a cash payment in their payroll check to reward inventors for the first-filed applications the company files. The amount of cash per invention and per application is capped and it is shared equally if the number of inventors exceeds five.

The program recognizes the individuals who have achieved any of the three stages of accomplishment on our company IP page, at quarterly awards events, and in congratulatory letters from senior executives to inventors and their coaches. Our CEO personally signs a congratulatory letter when a U.S. patent is granted and each inventor is presented with a patent coin along with the CEO's letter in a nice frame for display.

This Reward and Recognition Program now supports many new and innovative ideas that are focused on our businesses and that we believe will become very commercially important and valuable to Nielsen in the future.

Allen Lo, Vice President of Intellectual Property at Juniper Networks, explains how he determined the role for IP at Juniper as the first step toward relating the portfolio to the firm's business strategy and objectives:

I looked at our portfolio one day and asked 'What role does IP play in Juniper's business strategy?' Because at the end of the day, Juniper's business is selling products and services. IP is an adjunct to that business activity and so our IP strategy has to support the company's business strategy.

I was able to identify three ways in which the company used its portfolio of intellectual property. We were then, as we are now, very clear that as we build our portfolio, the choices we make about what patents are to be filed and what patents or other IP we buy need to be consistent with at least one of those three kinds of uses.

The first way we use our portfolio of IP is for counter-assertion purposes. We want to have a portfolio that is strong enough to allow us to push back against operating companies that come after us.

The second way Juniper uses its IP portfolio is to sustain competitive advantage. Our company believes that it has achieved some measure of competitive advantage through the very products and services it sells. Nevertheless, we want to utilize the patents as one more way to sustain that advantage. While our business activity, for example, may get us an early time-to-market, the company wants to see how we can extend and protect that advantage.

The third way our company uses its portfolio of IP involves protecting our products against someone trying to reverse-engineer them in order to clone them.

So, with the kind of value we seek to obtain from our portfolio now identified, we are able to focus it on specific ways it can contribute to the company's business strategy. This has advantages in building a strong and high-quality portfolio for

Juniper, but also for managing our portfolio in a cost-effective manner, as we can eliminate any patents that don't support the business, thereby eliminating all of their associated costs.

Best Practice 2: Create an Effective Screening Criteria

One of the most critical processes for Level Two companies is establishing a screening process and criteria for what goes into the patent portfolio. Patent screening is a common activity for cost-conscious companies. Whereas companies at Level One are often devoid of processes and formal decision criteria, companies at Level Two have come to realize that there is value in some degree of formality and process. While no one likes excessive process or mindless bureaucratic procedures, it is also true that people don't like to waste effort or be forced to rebuild a go/no-go patent decision procedure every time a new opportunity arises. Successful companies have learned that there are a number of key bits of information and core processes that can significantly improve both the efficiency and effectiveness of their patenting decisions. Information and systems need to be tailored to the companies' level of invention wealth. Some companies are "invention-poor"—that is, they do not spontaneously receive a sufficient number of inventions from their employees. Companies in this situation should be interested in creating processes and methods that encourage the creation of new inventions.

Other companies are "invention-rich"—that is, they receive more inventions from their employees than they can commercialize. These companies should be interested in creating screens and filters to identify the inventions of greatest interest to the firm. The point here is that not all best practices suit all companies at this level. Each company must diagnose its situation to determine which of the best practices cited in this chapter really relate to their circumstances. Screening patents should begin as early as possible. According to Arian Duijvestijn, GM of IP Lighting at Philips, "Start-up companies need good IP to help them obtain funding, whereas larger companies need good IP once they get into trouble with competitors." So how do companies implement a screening criteria process? Gene Potkay, SVP of IP at Nielsen explains his company's screening process:

As but one example, the fact that patents can be used to exclude leads many people to believe the only viable IP strategy is to use patents to pursue every last infringer that anyone might identify. That is not always a viable, sustainable, or immediate strategy for a commercial company. Reorientation of IP strategy to patenting for defensive purposes required getting back to basics. When you patent for defensive purposes, you do it to cover your own developments and areas that you expect could be valuable to your existing or potential future competition. As such, when forming your patent committee, the decision criteria to approve patent filing should be based on prioritizing candidates with the biggest potential commercial benefit to either you or your potential competitors. Certainly, looking ahead, you end up being able to; if you have the right people involved, enable the company to recognize potentially valuable inventions versus others that may be comparatively trivial.

Step 1: Before we bring invention disclosures to the patent committee, our in-house patent counsel will review the invention with a champion of the technology area who is familiar with the subject matter. They meet with the inventor(s) to assess the merit of the invention disclosure: whether it's novel, whether it's patentable, and whether or not it appears to have potential future value. If it clears those hurdles, it goes to the patent committee.

We ask the patent committee two questions and two questions only. We're not looking to have a technical discussion about it. We simply ask: Is it potentially commercially important to Nielsen or is it potentially commercially important to existing competitors or to our future competition? That's it.

On that basis, we know three things. We've got our view from a legal perspective on whether it looks patentable, whether it looks like it could clear prior art, and we have input from good subject-matter experts, leaders of the business, on whether it looks commercially important, and that's it.

Another important consideration for a screening criterion is the composition of the patent portfolio. Business managers usually want the portfolio to contain patents covering the products and services the company is or will be offering its customers. But this can lead to problems down the road. Erik Oliver of Sezmi explains, "Every time somebody asks 'Do our patents read on our products?,' I say that is not really a very interesting question. The more interesting question is, 'How well do our patents read on our competitors?' That is the billion-dollar question." And that is because your portfolio should also assist the company in dealing with its competitors. And it is always helpful to be able to pull out a number of patents that your competitor would find meaningful or useful to be able to assist with a negotiation or conversation with a competitor. So a screening criterion that allocates a certain percentage of the portfolio to patents relating to company competitors (either business or IP) is a useful criterion. As Jim O'Shaughnessy, of the consulting firm Percipience LLC, explains:

> The following chart describes the objectives I believe should animate patent strategies for any company [Figure 4.3]. To put the chart into words, it says that I strive to control or manage or influence my markets, sectors, and strategic relationships. In practice I want to place as many checks as possible in the nine boxes, recognizing that if I "control" a sector, for example, I will also be able to "manage" or "influence" it. Perhaps the most important insight I gained over time when using this approach is that there is no tenth box. If you are building a patent portfolio for any other reason, you are wasting resources.

Goals of the Ideal Portfolio

	Market	Sector	Relationships
Control			
Manage			
Influence			

Figure 4.3   Goals of the Ideal Patent Portfolio

I have found the relationship column to be very complementary to the market and sectors columns. I can choose to control or manage or influence my strategic relationships. Alternatively, if I don't control or manage or influence strategic relationships, then I can be relatively assured that I will be controlled or managed or influenced by one or more of them.

Of course, determining which strategic relationships make a difference or matter to me takes some time, but is a very worthwhile exercise.

So, for example, looking at a company like Whirlpool, their market is home appliances. The sectors or product lines might be things like kitchen appliances versus laundry appliances, and you can break it down even more into refrigeration or food preservation and clothes washers, clothes dryers.

That middle grouping allows you to pick the parts of the market that are the sweet spot of your interest. The first two columns, market and sectors, can be thought of as geography; I want to be operating in these places. The third column is relationships, which I mentioned earlier, but which actually inspired the chart. Relationships deal with markets based upon those who operate within them. Yes, they can be competitors, but there are also suppliers, there are customers, and there are complementors. Complementors are those companies that, when they sell their goods or services, pull or push the company's goods or services through the complementor's channel.

This leads to the importance of the premise that we make better decisions when we have the most informed position from which to make those decisions, and it is having a really clear understanding of what competitors are doing, what the markets are doing, that gives us an insight. So these objectives can help to build a strategy around a portfolio with three components—organic innovation, complementary innovation, and purchasing. When the above processes are completed with all of these background factors taken into account, one should have a portfolio that has very good offensive value, defensive value, and hedging value.

Best Practice 3: Manage the Patent Portfolio In a Cost-Conscious Manner

Patents are forward-looking. We like to say that patents are an option on a future value stream. An option is similar to a bet. So as you can imagine, if you place many bets regarding the future, not all of them will be winners. Patents precede products, which precede markets. The time between the filing of a patent application and having a product on the market can be anywhere from 2 to 10 years (depending on the technology area). During that time, many things can happen that cause the patent option to lose value. The technology doesn't work. The market doesn't materialize. A competitor creates a more compelling product. The list is endless. In all of these events, the patent option may no longer be high. So when we think of managing costs related to a patent portfolio there are two components: (1) the cost of determining what should go into the portfolio (screening) and then prosecuting the patents, and (2) the cost of maintaining and culling a portfolio once it has been created. As Kent Richardson, SVP, Business and Legal Affairs at Sezmi, points out:

> It is extremely important to review your portfolio regularly, so not only do you routinely screen it for valuable patents over time, but more important, you are looking for what patents can be abandoned or monetized. No company has unlimited funds for patents, so it is very critical to review the portfolio to separate the wheat from the chaff.

Gene Potkay of Nielsen addresses the latter process:

> Foreign filing is the gift that keeps on giving, so if you don't get that "right" early on, the costs can escalate, particularly if you don't go back and cut that down as you learn what's not important anymore. So directionally the best place to cut down on expense is making good decisions as early as you possibly can. You are never 100 percent right, so once you get to the point where the back end costs for all the filing, prosecution in foreign and maintenance fees begin to get out of control, you can set your sights on that problem. When I arrived at Nielsen, it was not apparent that a foreign filing strategy existed, considering

there were 37 countries in which Nielsen had filings. That's far more than what most company budgets can justify.

Even when an invention meets the general criteria a company sets for patentability, it is not always necessary to patent the invention in every major country, or renew it continuously in those countries. Uncontrolled filing and renewal can lead to excessive costs. For many companies, filing and maintenance fees can exceed 50 percent of a company's patent-related budget. Companies recognize, for instance, that the costs of filing and maintaining a patent in some countries may outweigh the minor benefits to be obtained there. The authors recall a story from an IP Manager in the 1990s. His company was filing in Colombia and he wanted to know why. He was told it was important to the strategy of the firm. He then went to the litigators and asked if any of them were willing to go to Colombia and enforce the patent. At that time guerrillas were known to kidnap foreigners and hold them for ransom. Every litigator declined to go to Colombia. They stopped filing patents there soon after. However, while patent protection may lose value in some countries, it may gain value in others. China used to be a country that many foreigners were loath to file in. Today, however, it is seen as a strategic necessity. When considering foreign locations, operations are an important consideration. Sophisticated companies also carefully consider those locales where they intend to employ the technology and avoid pursuing legal protection in areas of the world where they do not expect to operate.

Whether abroad or at home, the creation and maintenance of a patent portfolio involves joint decision-making across a number of functional areas including R&D, legal, and the business. Creating a standardized decision process involving all three groups and aggregating the necessary information for decision-making can be a daunting task. Since 2001, the amount and quality of IPM software options has increased and has made this task a little easier.

Gary Bender, Head of Global Intellectual Property at Visa, talks about how his group developed processes for managing the company's IP portfolios with a view toward minimizing costs:

> I was hired by Visa to create, implement, and manage processes
> for creating, capturing, and realizing the greatest possible amount

of business value from the company's intellectual property. I knew from my years of consulting in the field of IP management that anyone coming in from outside an organization needs to pay careful attention to the company's views about IP and its management, the company's culture, and the company's current processes for managing its intellectual property.

I learned that Visa has evolved a very effective way of managing its business. Because one of the company's major tasks is to handle massive amounts of data, and to do so in a zero tolerance for error manner, it has developed structures and processes that ensure that things are managed efficiently and on-time.

When I arrived on board I realized that I must add one more process to the company's existing way of doing things: an IP management process. I had to create it and then add it to the list of processes that everyone in the firm must comply with, or find the spot across the existing infrastructure of processes. I didn't at that time know whether to embed the IP management process within the Risk group's processes, the ERM program's processes, the sourcing program, or the technology development program, as they all have program management processes.

I quickly learned what these processes comprised, which ones worked well, and which ones were key processes that everyone used and were anchors across the company's management functions. That allowed me to understand where and how to insert the related IP requirements for my new process into processes people were already comfortable using. One of the benefits of this approach has been that I have been able to keep my team small while obtaining a broad reach throughout the company by using existing processes to the greatest extent possible.

I also needed to install an IP management information system in order to be able to manage the firm's broad range of intellectual property in a cost-conscious manner. I developed the specifications for the system I wanted for Visa so that I could take advantage of information and decision processes the company already had to offer. I explored a range of commercially available docketing systems, legal systems, tools, and databases, and learned something important. You can't install IP management software to manage your company's intellectual property if you are not already managing the company's intellectual property. In other words, you can't take a generic IP management system and use it as the basis for how you will manage your firm's IP.

I eventually decided on a software package where the vendor was willing and capable of modifying it to meet my specific needs for Visa. We are still in the process of bringing it up to speed in preparation for deploying it enterprise-wide. Once it is completely in place, I expect that the efficiency as well as the effectiveness of our efforts to manage the company's intellectual property for business value will be greatly enhanced.

Managing the patent portfolio holistically often requires continuous monitoring and vigilance. Kevin Donnelly, Senior Vice President of IP Strategy at Rambus explains:

I am sure that all companies have some kind of front-end patent committee and selection criteria. That's important, but it's the later patent development and ongoing management that makes a portfolio more valuable. We look at our portfolio on an ongoing basis (not just when we file), examining the changing market requirements and how the specifications of what we have filed align with these new requirements. We ask ourselves how we could make incremental improvements to our innovations by adding more parts of the solution or by changing it in some way to meet these evolving needs. This process of assessing and incorporating feedback from the market inherently will make an IP portfolio more valuable.

Best Practice 4: Begin Discussions Regarding "Make versus Buy" Innovation Preferences

The "make versus buy" patent decision is one that is handled very differently from one firm to the next. There are a number of factors involved in making this decision, and they vary by size of company, where the company is based on its development and growth curve, and also by industry.

Let's begin by picking up the thread we started in our discussion of Best Practice 1: Relate the portfolio to the company's business. Jim O'Shaughnessy, of Percipience LLC shares his view on the subject:

> When we look at a patent portfolio and perform a gap analysis we see that no matter how good the company, there are always gaps between what patents you have and what patents you realistically need. Not what you want, but what the portfolio must contain to deliver the value expected from it. There are three contributors to a well-rounded portfolio. One contribution, around 55 percent to 65 percent of a good portfolio, comes from organic innovation, which is all "make." Then there is complementary innovation, and the contribution from that source is typically on the order of 20 percent to 35 percent. It will vary from company to company, but not radically. The third source is purchase, and that would be what we're talking about when considering "make versus buy." This is the "buy." Organic innovation and complementary innovation are make; different forms of make, but they're both make. When we look at a portfolio, in my experience less than 10 percent should be contributed by purchasing, and often much, much less than 10 percent in a well-run, well-organized company operating in the United States or North America.
>
> But there are times when buying a patent or buying patents can be not only a very prudent thing to do, but essential. Typically what you're buying is time, but in a peculiar sense. You cannot invent something that is already invented or re-patent it, that's axiomatic, and so making something in the face of a lot of prior art may simply not be possible. However, you can go back into the issued patents and buy patents that are important or essential to your business that cover technologies important or essential to you, but which you cannot create yourself due to blocking prior art. That sometimes happens, and sometimes in those instances, you can purchase those patents for a reasonable sum of money. To me that's the simple case of buying patents. The more difficult buy, if you will, deals with technology inputs, and it's more than just patents that you're looking for.

Certain things drive a "make versus buy" decision, and I like to look at it as a matter of comparative advantage versus absolute advantage. So the first box to check is, Can we make this technology at all? and if we cannot, then we're talking about absolute advantage and not comparative advantage, and we need to deal with someone who can bring that technology to us. I'd say that's maybe at most 15 percent of the cases in which "buy" is the path forward, maybe a little bit more in some companies, a little bit less in others, but clearly the minority. It is more often a question of comparative advantage where my company certainly could "make," but for any one of a number of reasons would prefer to "buy." So in a strict comparative advantage situation I am better off devoting internal resources to other things. It may be to a more rapid development of the parts I am making, it may be to another program altogether, but there are other things that have a high enough priority that I would prefer not devoting resources, and typically human resources, to this project and prefer to find somebody who can do so for me.

It may be that it speeds my time to market by having someone else do certain things for me, and I'm thinking of the way that Boeing operates.[1] Boeing certainly has the capacity to make a wide range of the components that go into a modern aircraft, but they choose to outsource a lot of them in a "buy versus make" environment to give them the opportunity to devote their resources to other things that they prioritize higher. It may be a cost advantage, but more often I think it's a time advantage, an answer to the question of how we can assemble all of the technologies that we need to produce a complicated system and which subsystems or components ought to be outsourced, ought to be bought rather than made.

Juniper Networks' Allen Lo talks about the way they have implemented this best practice at Juniper Networks:

When we are considering where to obtain the patent coverage our company needs, we certainly take into account that some we can "make" ourselves, but some we ought to be able to "buy." When we looked at the three uses our company makes of the patents in our portfolio, we recognized that the nature of one of those uses was consistent with "buying" patent protection from outside the company, whereas two of those uses were much more consistent with developing patents internally.

Counterassertion is most likely to be against companies in fields within which we don't do development. In the past, we've made some efforts to file in areas outside of our core competencies, but have been less successful than we would have liked. Because of that experience, we are most likely to obtain patents for counterassertion use by purchasing them from others.

Patent protection for two other uses of our patent portfolio, sustaining competitive advantage and prevention of cloning, is most likely to come out of our own R&D efforts. For that reason, we will most likely seek to "make" patents for these two purposes rather than buy them from the outside.

The experience of Erik Oliver, VP of Legal Affairs at Sezmi, provides an interesting insight into the implementation of this best practice, this time at a start-up company:

The normal behavior for companies in the start-up stage of their development is to pursue both technology development and obtaining the patenting internally. They may hire outside counsel to assist with writing the patent, but that work is accomplished under the supervision of in-house counsel. This norm, the "make your own patents" norm, is a strong one. An alternative could be to purchase an existing patent, assuming it relates to your firm's business space and that the claims are supportive of your needs. Buying an existing patent might be cheaper; certainly it provides more immediate protection than does a patent application in process. There appears to be some kind of resistance in start-up firms to buying patent protection rather than making it. We observe that almost all start-up companies "make" their patents.

There appears to be an inherent paternalistic view about one's own patents that is not dissimilar to one's view of one's children . . . my own are cuter, smarter, more precocious . . .

Well, you get the point. People are simply more comfortable with their own creations. They believe they have a complete understanding of what they created versus buying a patent they do not fully understand. This psychological hurdle is one that companies usually get over as they become larger and gain more experience with the business world.

Interestingly, if you think about it, if you could buy a patent, then you could also sell one. In fact, the hurdle that companies need to clear involves make, buy, sell, and license, all together. Because once you do one of them, then it becomes easier to do the others.

Steve Baggott of P&G discusses how his firm implements the make versus buy decision:

Historically at P&G, looking externally had often been seen as a last resort, "I've tried everything I can. Let me go see what's available on the outside." Today it's common for our folks to look outside first. Chances are, somebody may have already developed the solution to what's keeping them up at night, or at least come close. The most efficient path to innovation is going to be trying to find some way of either accessing or building on the work that's already been done.

The key is to involve Connect + Develop resources in the very earliest logical phase of a project. That way, we can do the landscaping work to understand what's out there, what the options are, what the alternatives look like. If we don't find any viable assets, it could be that the search was imperfect, or maybe a solution doesn't exist which makes the "make versus buy" decision becomes pretty simple.

If, however, we find, say, five candidates for a particular technology challenge, we will run those through our screening and vetting process to determine if one or two would be the best fit. From there, the "make versus buy" decision becomes fairly objective. The key questions are around the value of accessing the external asset, which includes speed to market. We then need to consider how much do we need to pay to access it, and does that represent a cost-effective economic decision? We will do financial modeling to understand what's it likely going to cost, and we can compare that to doing it internally.

We try to have folks who can go out and do that process early, and if there are assets on the outside then we subject them to both screening and then financial modeling to determine whether there is a cost-effective option to try to bring in that capability at whatever appropriate stage that would be.

Once the company does clear the psychological hurdle, then "make versus buy" becomes a straightforward business decision and part of the company's standard practices.

Summary

Cost management brings clear benefits to organizations—including the benefit of decision-making clarity. But the journey to the boardroom does not end here. The many companies that have progressed beyond this level have learned they cannot concentrate only on the defensive and cost management levels of the value hierarchy. If they do, they will likely miss opportunities to capture maximum value from their IP. To seize such opportunities, companies need to progress to the next level: Level Three: Capture Value.

Chapter 5

Level Three:
Capture Value

Companies that have moved to Level Three have experienced an epiphany. They now realize that their intellectual property (IP) can be used as both a legal and a business asset. That is, it can provide business value beyond revenue derived from protected products and services. Whereas companies at Levels One and Two are focused largely on the defensive use of IP, companies at Level Three realize that they possess two kinds of value. The first are the company's innovations themselves—the ideas that yielded the products and services that generate the company's prime revenue stream. But in addition, Level Three companies realize that the IP itself has value—notably in tactical (rather than strategic) positioning, and in the profitable generation of new revenues (see Figure 5.1).

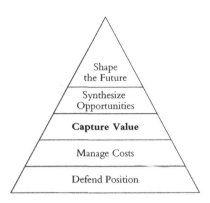

Figure 5.1   Level Three of the Value Hierarchy

What Level Three Companies Are Trying to Accomplish

Companies at Level Three see their IP as business assets, not just as legal ones. As business assets, the bits and pieces of a company's IP can become puzzle pieces in answering the great question: How can we succeed in building this company's value?

At this level, companies typically want to accomplish four things:

1. Identify the kinds of value they want from their IP.
2. Develop a value capture strategy.
3. Organize the company to capture value.
4. Develop IP reporting metrics.

Notice that we have changed the wording in a significant way. We used to think in terms of "extracting value" from intangibles. But over the years, it has become clear that companies are both creating and extracting value from their intellectual property. From the perspective of a company at Level Three, the activities and decision points in the top row of the IP Management System (IPMS) are closely associated with how the company plans to create value through its intellectual property, whereas the activities and decisions along the bottom row generally encompass what and how the company will go about converting IP into business value. Hence, we realize that Level Three companies are looking to capture the value of their IP.

It should also be noted that companies at Level Three have shifted the focus of their IP management (IP as a legal asset focused on risk reduction) toward business activity (IP as a business asset focused on value creation and value capture) that is concerned with the business use of the IP. Additionally, the previous two levels focused largely on IP generated internally, and now Level Three companies look at how value can be generated by IP owned by the company and IP to which the company has access from third parties. At this level, IP managers examine business opportunities to determine whether and how intellectual property might be helpful in converting the opportunity into captured value for the firm. Further, we see companies at Level Three concerned with their competitors' uses of IP as well as with how they might use their own IP to best tactical business advantage—all for maximum profitability in the short term.

Companies at Level Three have expanded the scope of their IP management activities beyond those needed solely for defensive purposes. Companies at the Level have created activities that allow them to capture a broad range of value from their intellectual property. The portions of IPMS they now care about include the shaded portions of Figure 5.2.

Best Practices for Level Three: Capture Value

Level Three companies are now moving past IP as a risk-reduction tool to one in which IP is now a value generator. This shift in utilizing IP as both a legal asset and a business asset is significant. For the first time, it allows the business manager to include IP as a value-generating asset in his or her tool kit and opens up a variety of ways that IP can generate value. Level Three companies adopt a series of best practices, often including these four:

Best Practice 1: Define the value to be obtained from the company's IP.
Best Practice 2: Develop an IP strategy to capture value.
Best Practice 3: Organize to capture value.
Best Practice 4: Develop metrics for IP reporting.

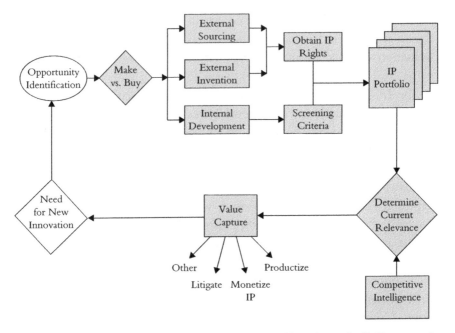

Figure 5.2 The IP Management System Showing Activities and Decisions Applicable to Level Three

Best Practice 1: Define the Value to Be Obtained from the Company's IP

Through the ICM Gathering we have learned that there are many different kinds of value that companies seek from their intellectual property. The specific kinds of value an individual company wants to obtain from its IP invariably differs from one company to the next.

The ICM Gathering companies have identified approximately 40 specific kinds of value that they actually obtain from their IP. The Gathering's list is not exhaustive, but it is representative of what companies may want from their IP (see Figure 5.3).

For IP managers, the kind of value that their own company wishes to obtain becomes a centerpiece objective of their firm's IP strategy. Arguably, if one doesn't know the kind of value one wants to obtain, it is difficult to create a viable strategy for obtaining it.

In the author's experience, most companies have not explicitly defined either one of two key elements that must underlie a credible IP

Defensive	Patents	Trademarks	Know-How	Relationships
Conflict Avoidance/ Resolution	• Protection (exclude others) • Design Freedom • Cross-Licensing (defensive) • Litigation Bargaining Power	• Protection (exclude others)	• Protection (trade secret)	N/A

Offensive	Patents	Trademarks	Know-How	Relationships
Revenue Generation	• *Products and Services:* Sales, Licensing, JV, Strategic Alliance, Optimization of Core Technology, Value Capture from Non-Core Technology, Integration, Donations • *Patents:* Sales, Licenses, Donations, Infringement Policing • Increased Bargaining Power (e.g., suppliers, customers, affiliates, JV/Alliance Partners) • Market Penetration • Increased Speed to Market	• *Products and Services:* Sales, JV, Strategic Alliance • *TM:* Sales, Licenses, Co-Branding, Infringement Policing	• Sales • Licenses • JV • Strategic Alliance • Integration • Increased Speed to Market	• *Products and Services:* Sales
Cost Reduction	• Litigation Avoidance • Access to Technology of Others • Improved Knowledge Transfer • Reduced Knowledge Gaps	• Litigation Avoidance • Access to Technology of Others	• Litigation Avoidance • Improved Knowledge Transfer	• Reduced Marketing Costs
Strategic Position	• Reputation/Image • Competitive Blocking (exclusivity) • Barrier to Competition • Supplier Control • Customer Control • Optimization of Core Technology	• Name Recognition • Customer Loyalty • Barrier to Competition • JV • Strategic Alliance	• Reputation/Image • Barrier to Entry	• Reputation/Image • Customer Loyalty • Barrier to Entry

Figure 5.3 Value Capture Options

strategy. The first is a definition of what "value" means to the company or, in other words, what it is that the company finds to be of business value. The second is the specific kinds of value that the firm wants to realize from its IP.

The significance of identifying the kinds of value the firm wants from its IP cannot be overemphasized. It is the bedrock on which a sound IP strategy is constructed. This best practice, "Defining the value to be obtained from the company's IP," is intertwined with Best Practice 2, "Developing an IP strategy to capture value."

On completing Best Practices 1 and 2, the IP manager should have:

- A list of all of the elements and subelements of the business strategy for which IP can provide support (see Best Practice 2).
- For each, a list of the kinds of support the IP function can provide (the kinds of value the firm wants from its IP).
- A list of the areas where IP efforts will *not* be a focus (although this is not to say that IP won't be used in any of these areas, only that IP resources will not be expended to create ongoing capabilities to do so).

Each ICM Gathering member company puts the above ideas into practice in ways that suit its company situation and organization best. Gene Potkay, SVP Intellectual Property at Nielsen, provides his perspective on the kind of value Nielsen wants to obtain from its IP and how this is determined:

> Nielsen is a company whose business is about measuring consumer interests and actions. Nielsen's reports and opinions are well respected and well received by our customers and by consumers at large. While this is the external view, or what outsiders see about our company, the internal view regarding how we make the measurements accurately and reliably is a bit different. We see ourselves as a technology company that focuses on sophisticated measurement techniques and analytics. Our internal research in these two areas is vital to keeping us on the cutting edge of measurement and analysis as it relates to consumers. We are continually upgrading our methods and techniques in order to maintain our reputation and the quality of our results. For Nielsen, its intellectual property is vital to

protecting its evolution in measurement and analysis as it proceeds down the technology highway.

Scott Frank, President and CEO of AT&T Intellectual Property, reports on how they define the value to be realized from their IP and how they go about it:

> At AT&T IP, our role is to strategically enhance AT&T's profitability with intellectual property. We facilitate the development of innovative ideas, convert AT&T's most valuable ideas into intellectual property assets, and determine the best ways to provide value in concert with the rest of the firm. As a group we are measured on our revenue generation. Additionally, we are also measured on cost savings we generate and other ways we utilize the portfolio to add profits to the bottom line. A good example of how we bring these different value-capture strategies together can be seen in a technology called "Watson." Watson is voice-recognition software that was created in our labs. We negotiated an IP license with an Internet search startup company, in return for an equity stake. We did that but made sure the license included a license back to AT&T for any and all improvements to the technology, and we also got customer data that was then fed back into AT&T Labs to update the technology. This allowed the Labs to have a third-party help develop the technology on their nickel with rights to all the improvements coming back to AT&T. In another example, we licensed the same Watson technology to a smart phone GPS navigation company. This company was providing an AT&T branded navigation app on smart phones and was interested in a flexible speech recognition interface. In the end, we licensed the Watson technology for revenue, and at the same time, helped the marketing organization to obtain better terms on the AT&T branded smart phone app.

Best Practice 2: Develop an IP Strategy to Capture Value

The word "strategy" is derived from the Greek word *strategos*, which translates as "the work of the generals." In modern military terms, strategies may be about creating force capabilities to defend against potential armed threats, providing military means to enforce national policies, developing weapons and supplies for those forces, and defining potential theaters of operation, as well as potential missions that forces may be required to carry out. Modern business strategies are analogous, although, of course, they deal with commercial activity instead of armed conflict.

Strategy differs from tactics. Whereas the former is concerned with how the war is to be won, the latter deals with how an individual battle is to be conducted. In business terms, strategy is what the company intends to do to reach its long-term objectives; tactics are the activities it pursues in specific business situations to meet short-term goals. While strategy is about positioning and capability development, tactics are about specific actions to resolve short-term problems.

The IP manager needs to understand the difference between strategy and tactics. Because an IP strategy should support the firm's business strategy, the IP manager needs to be able to define the major elements of the company's business strategy and be aware of, but not diverted by, the company's need for tactical IP support. Ideally, the IP manager should first develop an IP strategy to support the business's achievement of its long-term objectives. Having accomplished that goal, he or she can then turn to the company's tactical needs for IP support to learn whether the IP and IP value called for in the IP strategy are sufficient to also provide tactical support, or whether they need to be augmented by additional intellectual property.

The IP manager begins the process of developing an IP strategy by understanding the firm's *business* strategy. A good business strategy has five major elements:

1. **Arenas:** Where will the company be active (e.g., products, market segments, geographic areas, core technologies)?
2. **Vehicles:** how will we get there (e.g., internal development, joint ventures, licensing/franchising, acquisitions)?
3. **Differentiators:** How will we obtain our returns (e.g., lowest costs, premium pricing, service)?
4. **Staging:** In what sequence will we act and how fast will we go?
5. **Success Measures:** How will we win (e.g., image, customization, price, styling, product reliability)?

The above framework is enormously helpful for creating or for analyzing business strategies. It is also an excellent framework for creating and analyzing an IP strategy.[1]

Although there are many definitions of the term *IP strategy*, we like the following one:

An IP strategy is the collective set of decisions and activities an organization makes regarding the actions, the positioning, and the capabilities it seeks to achieve with its intellectual property in order to support its long-term business objectives.

Note that the definition has as its underpinning "supporting the organization's long-term business objectives." This is based on IP's status as a business asset with a broad commercial potential, not merely as a set of passive and defensive legal rights.

The elements of the IP Strategy should mirror those of the business strategy. Using the framework suggested for the business strategy, one would expect the elements of an IP strategy to feature the following:

- Arenas
  - Which business areas will IP not support?
- Vehicles
  - What forms of IP are to be managed (e.g., patents, copyrights, trademarks, other)?
- Differentiators
  - What mix of defensive and commercial support will IP provide?
  - What is our IP attitude/style (aggressive, passive, other)?
- Staging
  - What IP initiatives will we pursue?
  - In what sequence?
  - At what speed?
- Success Measures
  - What are the measures of success for IP?
  - How will we develop them?
  - How frequently should the measurements be made?

Arenas The *Arenas* are the parts of the company's business where it will concentrate its resources. In IP terms, the Arenas are where IP activity will be focused—and perhaps even more important, by omission, where the organization will *not* develop ongoing capabilities or expend company IP resources.

Because the IP strategy supports the company's long-term business strategy, its underlying logic must be based on the same long-term business aspirations and objectives. With this in mind, the IP strategy should open with a restatement of the company's long-term business thinking, including its mission, its vision for itself, and its long-term business objectives.

Identifying the Arenas of the IP strategy that can support the business strategy may provide insight into some aspects of the business strategy. Defining the IP Arenas is also instrumental in building a strong business rationale and logic for why the company needs intellectual property and the business roles it will play.

Vehicles In an IP strategy, the *Vehicles* describe two elements of interest: the kinds of intellectual property to be involved, and the kinds of IP resources and organizational capabilities needed to fulfill the roles defined in the arenas section. Here the IP strategist needs to develop lists of both the kinds of IP on which the strategy will focus and the capabilities needed to support them. The interplay between Arenas and Vehicles has several organizational implications.

The Vehicles section of the IP strategy should include a discussion of the kinds of IP to be managed. It needs to define what types of IP will be included within the scope of the IP strategy's efforts and state whether the focus will be mainly on prosecuting patents (assuming the company is rich in invention disclosures), or will also facilitate the creation of invention disclosures (assuming the company is disclosure-poor). The importance of trade secrets will also have to be covered, as will the extent to which trademarks are involved. Once the relevant IP has been identified, management decisions need to be made. For example, will core patents be managed by the IP function and noncore patents managed by an external law firm? Will the IP function focus exclusively on patents and related topics and contract out trademark management to an outside firm?

The IP management function will need capabilities of three kinds: (1) to create or obtain the needed IP, (2) to conduct the administrative work associated with a portfolio of IP, and (3) to manage the business uses of the company's IP. To determine whether the company already contains these capabilities in-house or needs to acquire them, the IP strategy should answer the following sets of questions:

- What capabilities are needed to create or obtain the kinds of IP on which the firm intends to focus? How will the appropriate IP be identified? What methods and processes are necessary to create or obtain the appropriate IP? What are the internal processes for doing this? Will all of the IP be created internally? If so, why? Will some of it be purchased or in-licensed? If so, why? How will each portfolio (kind) of IP be populated?
- What capabilities are needed to administer IP portfolios? All intellectual property requires some form of administration (some more, others less). How does the IP function intend to provide this administration? Will it be done in-house? Will it be provided via contracted services? Will a mix be used, depending on the IP involved? Will support for the creation of IP be different from follow-on support once the IP is in the portfolio?
- What capabilities are needed to manage the business uses of the company's IP? For each kind of commercial support defined in the Arenas section, how is each piece of IP being used by the business? How is this information recorded? More importantly, how is it maintained and kept up-to-date? How often will business reviews of IP be conducted, and who will be involved in the discussions? If elements of the IP strategy involve in-licensing or out-licensing, accounting and royalty management capabilities need to be considered.

Differentiators There are a number of ways in which companies can differentiate themselves with their IP strategies. Two of the most frequently occurring *Differentiators* concern the mix of commercial and legal focus, and the IP management style that the company adopts.

Concerning the mix of activity, many companies focus almost entirely on the legal aspects of intellectual property, housing their IP activity under the umbrella of the chief legal officer and staffing their IP management activity almost entirely with attorneys. Other companies have a balanced mix of activity using both defensive and commercial elements to their IP management function. Some of the latter companies have a formally designated chief intellectual property officer (CIPO) with business or business development training rather than a legal background.

Differentiation has a second major facet: the attitude or style the company adopts in the execution of its IP strategy. Attitude and style are often referred to as the informal "rules of the game." In multi-business-unit organizations, it is not unusual for the rules to differ from one business unit to another. While these rules are usually implicit, it is important that the IP strategy be quite explicit about the ways in which the IP function intends to conduct its business. For example, some organizations adopt a take-no-prisoners approach in their IP activities. Their legal tactics are confrontational, such that potential infringers and licensees are viewed as combatants, and are treated accordingly. In contrast, other companies may take an attitude of "We will be reasonable so long as you are reasonable." In other words some companies take a short-term view, trying to wring every nickel out of a business negotiation involving IP, while others may take a longer-term perspective, seeking win-win solutions that lead to strong relationships with the other parties.

Does your company's IP strategy require that your commercial activities be active or passive? Will you actively seek out opportunities both internally and externally, or will you wait until they are brought to you? What face will the IP function provide to the people with whom it interacts, both internally and externally?

Staging   The *Staging* section of the IP strategy should outline how the company intends to move from its *as is* position to its desired or *to be* condition. Inevitably there will be new assets to develop, new capabilities to create, and new relationships to forge. Staging addresses the sequencing and speed of major moves, as it is not possible, or even desirable, to move ahead on all fronts simultaneously or with the same degree of vigor.

Practical constraints, such as budgets and manpower, usually dictate the rate at which events can proceed. The IP strategy specifies the focus, sequencing and speed of movement concerning activities such as the

creation of necessary capabilities or the sequencing and speed of movement concerning activities such as the creation of necessary capabilities
or the sequencing of providing selected kinds of support for selected
business Arenas with the goal of maximizing the value of the IP to the
business. For each element and subelement of the IP strategy, the Staging
section should specify the necessary actions, in what order, and on what
schedule.

Perhaps one of the more challenging aspects of this element of the
IP strategy involves determining which actions are initiating actions and
which actions are followers. This seemingly easy task is made difficult by
the intrinsic intertwining of actions. For example, conducting facilitated
invention creation sessions with technical teams makes little sense unless
there is a procedure in place to process the resulting disclosures.
Thinking through the interdependencies of various actions will enable
the IP strategist to get the horse before the cart and have several carts
progressing in sequence.

Success Measures   To gauge how well the IP function is progressing, in addition to how well it is supporting the business, most companies require periodic reports to address both sets of initiatives. In a
recent survey of the IP reporting practices of ICM Gathering companies,[2] there were several findings of potential interest:

- The study found that the nature and content of IP reporting has
  changed very little over the past decade, particularly in the format,
  style, and frequency of reports. The content of the reports has
  evolved somewhat, with the more sophisticated reports focusing
  crisply on the pertinent business issues with which IP is associated.
- Regarding the contents of IP reports, the study found that these
  might be categorized at the highest level as Simple Metrics, Complex Metrics, or Narrative Content (see Best Practice 4: Develop
  Metrics for IP Reporting).
- The strongest finding of this study was that the reporting of IP
  activity is particularly highly correlated with the degree of importance of intellectual property to the company's business, which in
  turn tends to be closely related to the degree of sophistication of the
  company's IP management. The correlations included the content

of the IP reports, the balance between metrics and narrative in the report, to whom the reports were sent, and the frequency with which the reports were submitted (see Figure 5.4).

- The study also found that organizations report in different directions: upward along the lines of the corporate hierarchy; sideways to R&D, Finance, and Business Unit Managers; as well as downward to the general corporate population.

Recipients of IP Reports   For companies at the higher levels of the Value Hierarchy pyramid, upward reports are always made to a C-Suite level executive or to the CEO directly. Companies positioned at the first two levels of the hierarchy send IP reports to an executive who may or may not be in the C-Suite; in no case did any company at the lower two levels report its IP activity directly to the CEO. Reports were typically sent to the Chief Legal Officer, or to the Chief Technology Officer, depending on where the IP Manager's unit resided within the company's organizational structure.

Lateral reports, usually containing the same content as the upward reports, are generally made to the Business Unit Managers (with detail associated with the Business Unit), and to the Chief Financial Officer.

Although the IP Managers surveyed did not see themselves reporting downward, each acknowledged that there was a significant

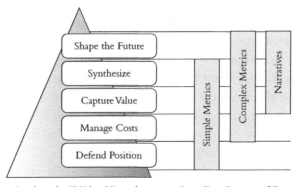

Figure 5.4   IP Report Contents at Each Level of the Value Hierarchy Pyramid

amount of information routinely communicated to employees at large, either through talks, memos, or IP newsletters.

Best Practice 3: Organize to Capture Value

In the original Edison we noted that at Level Three, once companies have determined the kinds of desired IP value, they then need to organize the group to capture that value. At this level the activities that support IPM cut across a variety of functions: legal, R&D, marketing, finance, and strategic planning. How do companies decide what decisions are made at the business unit level and at the corporate level? To help the IP manager sort through alternatives that might work at his or her company, we created an Authority and Activity Matrix, which can be seen in Figure 5.5.

The matrix results from a series of questions and answers that associates in a company's IP organization must pursue. Initial elements in this series are questions about the company's long-term vision and where it is going. The answers to these questions trigger the next question in the series: What is the company's strategy for achieving this vision? Following the answer to this question, one must ask: What are the roles (kinds of value) for IP in helping the company enable this strategy (see Figure 5.3)? The roles, once known, allow the company to determine which functions (see Figure 5.2) must be performed. Once the functions to be performed are known, the company can then ask itself how it wishes to organize to perform them.

In our experience, there are two areas of consideration when companies debate the question of centralization versus decentralization. The first concerns the authority to make important decisions, such as when to release any IP documents or matters to parties outside of the company; the second concerns the activities associated with the IP management functions themselves.

As can be seen in Figure 5.5, there are at least nine different possibilities we have identified for centralizing or decentralizing either or both the authority for IP management and its activity. For each company seeking to organize itself to manage its intellectual property, the decision of how best to organize will depend upon a number of factors, but often most importantly on the corporate and organizational cultures.

Activity

	Decentralized	Mixed	Centralized
Centralized	• Value capture may or may not be strategic to the firm. • IP activity fully dispersed throughout the BUs. • All value capture efforts are approved centrally.	• Value capture is not entirely strategic to the firm. • Value activities are shared: legal and licensing tend to be centralized, other functions are decentralized.	• Value capture important to corporate strategy. • All IP activities are under one roof (business and legal). • All value capture efforts are approved centrally.
Mixed	• Value capture is probably not strategic to the firm. • IP activity fully dispersed throughout the BUs. • Some forms of authority given to BUs, others reside within corporation.	• Value capture is not entirely strategic to the firm. • Value activities are shared: legal and licensing tend to be centralized, other functions are decentralized. • Some authority given to BUs, other resides with Corporate Staff.	• Value capture is not entirely strategic to the firm. • All IP activities are under one roof (business and legal). • Some authority given to BUs, other resides with corporate staff.
Decentralized	• Value capture is not strategic to the firm. • IP activity fully dispersed throughout the BUs. • Value capture is approved and released by BUs.	• Value capture is not entirely strategic to the firm. • Value activities are shared: legal and licensing tend to be centralized, other functions are decentralized. • Value capture is controlled and approved by BUs.	• Value capture may or may not be strategic to the firm. • All IP activities are under one roof (business and legal). • Value capture is controlled by BUs. All value capture is approved by BUs.

Authority

Figure 5.5   Degrees of Activity and Authority Centralization

The Chief Intellectual Property Officer In the course of the past decade, there has been a new concept that has emerged under the banner of organizing to capture value: the chief intellectual property officer, or CIPO. Originally conceived and popularized by Ron Laurie of Inflexion Point Strategy, the concept has been the topic of discussion at conferences and in publications for the past several years. Briefly, the CIPO is a person with business or business development training whose function involves the overall management of the firm's portfolios of intellectual property both for commercial as well as for legal value. In many cases, this person has a dotted line relationship with the company's legal department in dealing with matters of litigation.

Gary Bender is the Head of Global Intellectual Property at Visa and discusses his role as the company's CIPO:

> I manage the patents and technology and trade secret aspect of Visa's intellectual property. I do not manage the trademarks and brands associated with the organization. I was brought into the company just after the IPO of Visa in 2008 to take the intellectual property program of the newly combined global entity at Visa and evolve it to a coordinated and scaled program commensurate with the needs of the company and the growth and opportunities and new products the company was developing. The first question I get from most people that I meet, whether industry peers or even internal folks is, "Are you an attorney?" The answer is no. I have 15 years of intellectual property experience as an economic damages expert, as a consultant for intellectual property strategy that included patent portfolio analysis, licensing, due diligence, and strategic organizational design for managing IP. In fact, Visa International was a client of mine in 2003, which really led me to understand and get to know the company, which ultimately led to my role currently. It is a unique situation; it is a unique construct to have the head of intellectual property not be an attorney and also not be in the legal department. Both of those things, from my perspective—and I'll say this in an unbiased manner—I feel are advantages for me and the program and for Visa.
>
> Number one, I do bring a different, more business-aligned strategic way of thinking about intellectual property and patents,

licensing, and our interaction with third parties, whether it be in partnerships or M&A. My background clearly comes from the business and economics side, but with 15 years of experience in patent law and IP law and litigation; I can marry the two quite well. That lets me really focus on the business needs and the end results and expectations and goals that we're looking for. I have a team of people who are also not attorneys and who support me on analysis and deal due diligence and the patent portfolio, but I also have great paralegals and great attorneys, within Visa and externally, who obviously bring the legal horsepower when we need it.

Not being within the legal department offers some advantages as well. From the top down at Visa, they understand that—and because we're structured in that manner—outside of legal—we're looked at differently. They understand the value that IP and the program that I've developed and am managing bring to the company. Yes, it's expensive; yes, we're spending more since I've joined and continue to scale as the company scales globally, and the programs are scaling, but because we are very close with the nonlegal executives—products, strategy, and technology, and we interact with them regularly—they see the value that we're bringing and the partnerships that we're helping them form. They see that it is really part of the business. It's an instrument that is a very critical part of business today, as the concepts that we're working on and developing and rolling out are in a very competitive area—increasingly competitive, from the Visa standpoint. There is a wide respect for IP rights, internally and externally from the top down, and they realize that we should be looking at our IP position primarily from a business standpoint.

Dr. Seungho Ahn of Samsung Electronics talks briefly about his position as CIPO:

My role as CIPO of Samsung Electronics is to help the businesses better manage IP risks and to think more strategically about IP. My group is a corporate function with four groups reporting to me: IP licensing, IP legal, IP analysis, and IP strategy. I report to both the CFO and CEO. My role is Samsung Electronics' first attempt to centralize IP decisions and activities within the firm. Much of my time is spent coordinating IP matters between and among our various business units. My main objective is to protect Samsung's businesses from IP risk and hedge against risks through licensing, patent purchasing, and finding new technologies and IP to bring into the businesses.

Fifteen years ago Samsung's IP portfolio was negligible. Today it has grown to such a large scale that many companies are interested in cross-licensing with us. Our recent cross-license agreement with IBM is a good example of that. We have spent the past 10 years patenting very aggressively (we have been the number two top patent filer in the USPTO for the past five years and in the top 10 for the past 10 years). Currently Samsung is the largest electronics company in the world in revenue terms. As you can imagine that makes us quite a large target for NPEs. I am continually assessing and refining my strategies and responses to NPEs in the hopes that I can stay ahead of them and their ever-changing business models. But it is a relentless task. IP is more strategic for us today as it involves more money than ever before. Previously we were at the bottom of the Edison pyramid, just trying to build up an IP portfolio. But as our business has grown, so has our need to move up the pyramid and think more strategically about IP and how to use it to benefit our businesses. Certainly our business has grown and increased in complexity and the IP issues have followed suit requiring more strategic thinking and also a more corporate-wide view. To maintain our current growth requires new business opportunities and markets, and we are looking to utilize IP in more strategic ways to do that.

Ruud Peters, CEO of Philips Intellectual Property & Standards (IP&S), shares with us a little about his organization and structure:

IP has been around for more than a century at Philips. We received our first patent in 1905. Historically, we used patents defensively. However, in the 1970s the group began some licensing activities, which grew in the 1980s and 1990s until licensing was quite sizable. When I took over responsibility group in 1999, I realized that if we wanted to maximize our revenues, we had to manage our activities more professionally. Therefore we introduced process and project management and also began to grow the group. Early on, we established offices in emerging market countries, like China and India. We also brought all IP and IP-related activities and support groups, which sometimes were spread over the company, into the IP organization so that we had everything under one roof. For example, the financial licensing administration was part of the accounting department. By bringing this group into the IP organization, we could have the licensing and financial people work more closely together, which increased the efficiency of our licensing activities and had a positive impact on our revenues. In addition, we started new activities, like an anti-counterfeiting group in Asia. In 2001, we became a business with profit and loss (P&L) responsibility instead of being a cost center. This had a huge impact on the organization. It allowed everyone to be fully focused on creating value. It also allowed us to become more business-focused and more customer-focused. We also started to use our IP portfolio more as an asset, which could be used in multiple ways to create value. This allows us to focus on the total value captured instead of just doing licensing for money. During this transformation process we also changed our name from "Patents & Trademarks" to Philips Intellectual Property & Standards (IP&S).

IP&S has around 450 full time equivalent (FTE) employees. We are distributed over 16 countries with a presence in every region, but a particularly strong emphasis in Asia. Our structure reflects the structure of the company, which is divided into four sectors; health care, lighting, customer lifestyles, and corporate technologies, which includes the research and design centers. We have developed a flexible organizational model, which allows us to quickly adjust our organization when the company structure changes, which has happened a number of times in the last ten years. The IP&S organization has an outstanding change management capability which allows us to adjust rapidly to any changes, whether inside or outside of Philips.

IP&S is responsible for managing its operations and driving the activities to create value for the sectors and for the company. Within IP&S we have a wide range of people and functions such as a business intelligence group, a finance department, a human resources department, the communication department, the IP analyst groups, and our own legal group, which supports our business activities.

And finally, Ron Laurie, one of the first to socialize the CIPO concept and a founding Principal of both Percipience LLC and Inflexion Point Strategy LLC, comments:

It seems to me that today there are various flavors of CIPO depending on the corporate environment. The first is found in companies that are focused both on managing IP risk *and* on exploiting IP value-extraction opportunities. Examples of companies with this kind of CIPO are Philips, AT&T, and Samsung.

Another kind of CIPO is found at companies that are not concerned with IP monetization, but nevertheless see IP as being very strategic to their business model and markets. The CIPO's primary role in these kinds of companies is to manage (i.e., reduce) the company's IP risk exposure. Nielsen, Juniper, and Broadcom are examples of this type of CIPO.

And then there are CIPOs at companies where IP is the "product," such as Rambus, Tessera, and MOSAID. These companies typically have active internal R&D organizations—thus distinguishing them from non-practicing entities (NPEs) that acquire and enforce existing patents—and generate innovative semiconductor chip and chip packaging designs in digital form. These companies typically define IP as including both the designs (e.g., IP cores) and the associated proprietary rights (including patents, trade secrets, copyrights, and mask works) and they license both the designs and the use rights to their customers, often bundled with technical support in integrating the designs into the customers' products and processes. Some companies start out as IP companies and others transition from being a product company to an IP company. Qualcomm is a good example, having started out as a chip set company (which it still is), but with most of its profits now coming from IP licensing. The usual reason for this transition is that the margins in an IP licensing business model are much more interesting and attractive than the margins associated with selling physical products.

Each of the three types of companies occupies its own unique point on the risk management/value extraction spectrum. The closer a company is to the risk end of the spectrum, the more likely it is that the IP function will be contained within, and controlled and managed by the legal infrastructure. The closer it is to the value-extraction (a broader term than monetization) end of the spectrum, the more likely it is that the CIPO will be someone with corporate development, business management, or financial experience and will interact more frequently with the other business executives in the company.

Best Practice 4: Develop Metrics for IP Reporting

Since the early days of the management of IP, firms have struggled to find a good, if not an ideal, set of metrics to report on their progress toward goals as well as their processing activities. Early on there were a number of suggested lists of IP metrics proposed by one author or another. Over the past decade, however, several things have become clear. First, the decision on which metrics an IP manager is required to report resides not with the IP Manager but with his or her reporting seniors as well as with the people he or she reports to laterally.

It is also the case that virtually all firms, regardless of their level on the IP Value Hierarchy, tend to include the firm's simple metrics in their recurring routine IP reports. Before proceeding further, let us pause to define what we mean by metrics and what they comprise.

Fundamentally, IP managers are almost always tasked with providing routinely recurring reports that highlight key portions of their activity. These reports typically include measures of *process* and sometimes measures of *progress*. The reports may include purely quantitative information or some mix of quantitative and narrative information.

There are two kinds of qualitative data or "metrics" that may be reported: simple and complex.

Simple Metrics Simple metrics are basic counts of demographic information. They contain either or both just numbers or numbers per unit of time (week, month, year, etc.). Examples of simple metrics include:

- Number of patents, or trademarks, or copyrights in the company's portfolio.
- Number of invention disclosures per unit of time.
- Number of patent applications per unit of time.
- Number of patents granted.
- Number of patents granted per unit of time.

Complex Metrics Complex metrics relate intellectual property to some business activity of the company. They are more informative about the impact of IP on company business activity than simple metrics, but require more sophistication to generate. Examples of complex metrics include:

- Number of invention disclosures/patent applications/grants organized by business unit, or product line, or technology, etc.
- Licensing revenue, possibly differentiated by business unit, product line, or technology.
- Pace of patenting versus competitors, or by product line, or by business unit, or by technology.
- A taxonomy which links IP to the products and services it covers.

Complex metrics often require graphs or diagrams to convey their meaning, as well as brief narrative explanations accompanying the graph or diagram.

We would be remiss if we did not add one more category to reporting "metrics." That is the qualitative or narrative that is sometimes added to highlight key points relating to a specific IP-related business or legal issue. Qualitative Narrative in IP reporting is particularly important for companies at the higher levels of the Value Hierarchy. These narratives, usually in bullet-point format, briefly identify the issue and provide current information about its status. The IP reports for companies at the higher levels of the pyramid tend to have more qualitative or narrative information than metric information. For companies at the lower levels of the pyramid the reverse is usually the case.

Gary Bender, Head of Global Intellectual Property at Visa, discusses his view of IP reporting metrics:

> There are a slew of metrics you can generate with intellectual property, both looking internally and externally. You can drown in them and you can drown others in them if you need to or want to. But what we've found to be very, very helpful and what I do is a quarterly and annual IP executive report that goes to our operating committee and executive management teams and our leadership globally, which gives both an internal and external view. It gives qualitative comments on some of the internal activities, the IP program it's supporting and/or leading for the company, and it shows some external publicly available statistics around what we're doing, what others in the industry are doing, where they're doing it from a patent filing perspective, foreign, domestic, litigation activity—really just pretty straightforward stuff. It's very helpful to put things in context when you look internally and externally. Then we provide them with, obviously, some of the product-by-product activity, trends, innovation activities, patent filings, and those sorts of things, which give not only each of the business unit leaders visibility into how I'm investing in their business, but also how their business is participating in the innovation development and IP protection program. IP metrics and reports serve another great purpose as a reminder that, hey, by the way, we're here. We're supporting the business; keep it top of mind, a refresher that this is something that's important to the company. We're investing in it, and here's the latest. Each quarter we get questions from various parts of the organization, whether from the CFO, or from the CEO, or from our leader in Asia. It's

always productive and it helps show that we're supporting the business; we're aligned with the business and that we're teamed up together.

Ruud Peters, CEO of IP&S at Philips, discusses his view of IP reporting metrics:

Because we are a business with our own P&L responsibility, we are held accountable for our activities. Of course, we have the standard financial metrics such as revenues, cost, EBIT, cash flow, and net operating capital. That is part of our standard reporting and we report that on a monthly basis. Additionally, we have quarterly review meetings with the board of management where we discuss not only the financials, which we call the cash benefits, but also the non-cash benefits (which are cash benefits in the P&L of the businesses specifically due to IP). We express these non-cash benefits in financial terms such as euros (the currency in which we do our accounting). Together, they are the total value that we contribute to the company, a key measure for us. So, we not only look at revenues but also at all of the other value we generate through IP, and we add that all up. Because we express everything in financial terms, we can generate a total picture in financial terms, which our board understands better than non-monetary, more IP-related terms. At IP&S we believe that each and every activity that we undertake should generate value, and thus for each activity, we have developed models to express the resulting value in monetary terms. We determine what portions of the premium profits of specific products are due to IP and whether the cost savings per product are due to favorable IP transactions, which lower the bill of material for the business. Did IP help shorten a product's time to market, or did it help secure a market share increase? In addition to the financial metrics, we have input/output and process management metrics for each of our business activities to make sure that we meet our output targets and run the organization in an efficient manner.

Summary

With aggressive attempts to capture the value created by the firm's intellectual property, while at the same time reducing costs, IP-rich companies can emulate Thomas Edison's slow but sure journey to the boardroom. But we still have further to go. Profits are not everything, and we still haven't arrived at the boardroom door. More levels are ahead—including the Synthesize Opportunities level, the next tier on the IP Value Hierarchy.

Chapter 6

Level Four: Synthesize Opportunities

Companies that have achieved Level Four have come to understand the strategic implications of intellectual property (IP) for their firm. They look beyond defense, costs, and profits (see Figure 6.1). They realize that IP can be used to position them broadly in their marketplace as well as provide tactical positioning. They also see that IP may be used as an effective weapon against competitors. While profits may be made directly from their IP through monetization, companies at Level Four realize there are still greater opportunities. IP is now viewed as an integrated business asset that can be used in a broad range of ways: as a negotiating tool, as a way of positioning the company strategically, or even as a way of affecting the company's stock price.

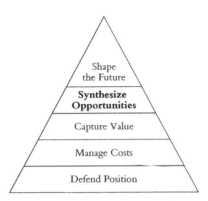

Figure 6.1 Level Four of the Value Hierarchy

In addition, the Synthesize Opportunities level marks a shift in the nature of the IP function. At this level the IP function begins looking outside its own walls to synthesize its expertise and resources with those of the rest of the company. It becomes more innovative and looks for ways to help other parts of the organization reach their goals.

What Level Four Companies Are Trying to Accomplish

Companies at Level Four have learned that the very ownership of IP brings with it a set of risks that must be balanced against the IP's potential rewards. Level Four companies begin to manage their IP more holistically, now being able to identify all or almost all of the compromises between IP, the dollar costs of IP, the risks of IP ownership, the revenue opportunities from IP, and the business benefits available from IP. At this level, companies typically want to accomplish two things:

1. Understand and capitalize upon the relationship between invention and innovation for the enterprise.
2. Help quantify the IP risk/reward trade-offs resulting from ownership of the organization's intellectual property.

At Level Four, companies are involved with the same component functions of the IP Management System, as are companies at Level

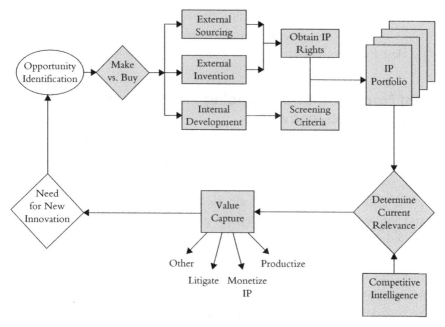

Figure 6.2 The IP Management System Showing Activities and Decisions Applicable to Level Four

Three. The difference is that at Level Four, the focus is at a greater degree of depth (see Figure 6.2).

Best Practices for Level Four: Synthesize Opportunities

In Levels One through Three, companies have been utilizing IP in fairly traditional ways, either aiding in risk reduction or generating additional value. Level Four companies begin to evaluate how IP can help drive change in their organizations, such as open innovation or new revenue models. To do so, however, requires some questioning of how the firm currently operates, and whether and how IP can add value. Gathering companies have defined two best practices that will enable companies to discuss how they can and should utilize IP. They are:

Best Practice 1: Understanding the relationship between invention and innovation.

Best Practice 2: Managing IP risk/reward trade-offs.

Best Practice 1: Understanding the Relationship between Invention and Innovation

In 2001, when *Edison in the Boardroom* was first published, one of the most novel concepts in the book was that IP could be used as both a legal asset (to minimize risk) and as a business asset (to maximize value). At the time, patents were typically tied to the company's core business (and innovations); the legal defense and business use of patents were focused accordingly. Since then, the IP ecosystem has undergone a dramatic expansion based upon these principles (see Appendix C). Although the IP ecosystem is in a continual state of evolution, we believe that it is currently out of balance. The focus over the course of the past decade has moved away from the defense or use of patents as part of their business activity to an emphasis on outside entities buying and selling intellectual properties as if they were a commodity—and defending or using them on that basis. The courts, certainly in the United States, are struggling with managing the number and variety of IP-related cases as well as questioning their own methods for assessing damages. The world's patent offices are struggling to find ways of dealing with a serious backlog of applications, improving their efficiency while maintaining their effectiveness and credibility as grantors of patents. The participants in the latter set of activities have lost sight of the relationship between patented invention and innovation.

Another important concept that arose in the original edition of *Edison in the Boardroom* was that IP has value in context. That means that the same IP will have different values depending on the owner or user. Even two firms in the same industry will capture different value streams from the same IP because their context and complementary business assets, strategies, and market positions are different, thereby providing different contexts in which the IP will be utilized.

So why is this? First, it proves that there is no "fair market value" for patents. Their value depends more upon how their owner intends to use them and what assets the owner brings to the party. The lack of a fair market value has obvious implications for both legal and business reasons. Second, the power of context casts doubt on the wisdom of commoditization. If the true value of patents is inextricably combined with the assets, strategy, and market position of their owners, then patents clearly lose value when separated from that context. Finally, the importance of context proves that invention and innovation are two very different concepts—a point that seems to be lost on our courts and policy makers. They frequently use these two terms as if they were synonymous, and they are not. Conflating invention and innovation can sometimes have counterproductive results. Ron Laurie explains:

> In the United States litigation environment, the usual measure of patent infringement damages is a "reasonable royalty." However, current methodologies for computing a reasonable royalty often have the effect of taxing a company's investment in innovation rather than compensating the patent owner for the unlicensed use of the patented invention. To get from a patented structure, function, or feature to a marketable product requires a number of steps beyond the mere "reduction to practice" (i.e., technical operability) that is required to get a patent, and each of these additional steps may involve a significant amount of capital investment. The first step is to combine the patented invention with other enabling technologies, some of which may themselves be patented. Then, this enabling technology often must be supplemented with manufacturing technology in order to convert a prototype into a commercially acceptable product. Finally, it is necessary to incur advertising and sales expenses to create a new market or to enter an existing market for the product. All of this expense, plus some profit, must then be recouped from the sales price. Under existing judicial approaches to reasonable royalty computation, the sales price of the commercial product is often used as the royalty base. The royalty rate applied to the base is "adjusted" (i.e., reduced) to compensate for all additional investment over and above the creation and reduction to practice of the patented invention, that is necessary to generate the sales price. This kind of fuzzy math is now under intense pressure in U.S. courts and we can

expect to see a more rational approach to damages emerging in the near future.

The concept of a spectrum ranging between patented *invention* at one end and *innovation* at the other also has implications for how companies conduct their R&D programs. Procter & Gamble has looked at its business and recognized that P&G's strength in innovation may be greater than its considerable strengths in invention. Steve Baggott explains:

> When A. G. Lafley came in as CEO in 2000, P&G's stock price had suffered significantly over the preceding quarters. He knew that there were a number of focus areas to get the company moving in the right direction. Some of those included concentrating on big countries and big customers, getting back to recognizing "the consumer is boss" and spotlighting big wins. He also thought we needed to be much more externally facing, so he committed himself and the Company to Open Innovation. He announced that P&G would get to the point where 50 percent of our initiatives were powered by external innovation.
>
> Some people at other companies view Open Innovation as an outsourcing of R&D effort, as a way to cut costs. That wasn't the intent at P&G when we embraced Open Innovation. We invent quite a lot internally—typically more than any of our competitors—but where we really excel is at putting those inventions together into a branded innovation that truly delights the consumer. With that realization, we began our journey of Open Innovation, which we have branded Connect + Develop.
>
> During our early days of Connect + Develop, we would seek out whatever our internal colleagues wanted. We learned the hard and painful way to be a bit more discerning. That included focusing our resources on opportunities that were strategically important to P&G, or that were globally aligned with a business unit's strategy.
>
> What we have learned about searching externally for new product opportunities is that they must be strategically aligned with one of our businesses, and, very importantly, there need to be

identified resources and funds and capability, such that when we bring potential solutions back, the business is ready to do something with them. What tends to be toxic for open innovation is going out and finding an opportunity, getting people on the outside to put forward what they would like to do, then bringing it back and hearing the business say, "Well, we really weren't that interested in that," or "I don't have any resources to make it work," or "Please tell them no, thank you, not now." You do that several times and people really don't have much interest in working with you. We have gotten much more intentional, strategic, and directed in our Connect + Develop efforts.

In addition, there is a critical part of Connect + Develop that is just smart serendipity. We have about 25 people around the world, including people in innovation hotspots like the Silicon Valley area and people based in emerging markets in Asia—in China, Korea, Singapore, and everywhere in-between. We have certainly seen with Connect + Develop that there are times we find something outside that does not speak to a specific and articulated need of the business—because, understandably, they don't know what they don't know. Because we have enough foresight into their strategies, we're able to bring those serendipitous connections back and say, "We know you didn't ask for one of these, but here is what we have found and we think this would be a wonderful fit with this innovation strategy that we know you have in your business."

Then the business can decide whether or not they wish to progress, but it's really a "both/and." It's very direct and strategic and need-based searching, but it's also being connected enough externally that we are open to serendipity, to tripping over things that are out there, then having a seamless way to quickly bring those back in and have them be considered at the right level within the business. People have developed a wide enough lens to be able to say, "That's interesting. I didn't know I needed one of those, but that looks like I should really redirect some resources to explore whether it makes sense."

When P&G has tended to stray it has been when we've fallen in love with technology that didn't have a clear route to delighting the consumer. We have lots of examples of things that never saw the light of day, nor should have, but there was a really cool technology behind them. By putting the consumer back at the center, we can be more agnostic about whether the innovation is internally or externally generated. Because the consumer doesn't know, and doesn't care. That has been a truly liberating and empowering concept. If we recall, what the consumer is paying for is whether or not we are delighting her, giving her a delightful experience, not that we've got 27 patents behind that particular product. In summary, we have found that the combination of focused external searching for strategically aligned opportunities as well as serendipitous opportunity identification have brought P&G many new ideas that we have been able to successfully innovate.

Whereas P&G innovates around physical products and uses them as its primary source of revenue and profits, Rambus is concerned with intangible products and has a very different perspective on the invention versus innovation issues, as Kevin Donnelly, Senior Vice President of IP Strategy, explains:

> Rambus is an intellectual property and technology licensing company. There are two parts to our business: patent licensing and solutions licensing. On the patent side we license our inventions; and on the solutions side we license complete technology solutions. Rambus focuses on creating technologies, architectures and inventions for digital electronics products and systems. Our business model has three key elements: invent, drive adoption, and license (the latter two together are what The Gathering calls the "innovation" portion of our strategy).
>
> Invention for us involves looking out into the future and developing innovations that provide solutions to difficult problems for semiconductors and other kinds of digital electronics and systems (we have traditionally focused on system-level problems).
>
> One may think of Rambus' early days as the first phase of its business model evolution. During that first phase, our business model was to license technology solutions, and we delivered

innovations to many companies simultaneously. This enabled as many as 15 companies at a time to bring the same product to market compatibly. At that time we called our approach "centralized R&D." The idea then was to drive adoption of our solutions across a large number of companies at once.

Later, we entered the second phase of our business model evolution, which involved a mix of licensing our inventions and licensing our solutions. Our aim is to license our technology, whether patents or solutions, as broadly as possible. We look for big problems, the solutions to which can bring large system-level benefits. After we create inventions, we drive adoption by communicating their advantages through performing demonstrations, writing specifications, presenting papers at conferences, and working directly with customers. Then we license our technology to customers in the way that best meets their needs, either through patent licensing or solution licensing.

We are now beginning to work our way into the third phase of our business model. In this phase, we believe we can take our patent and solution licensing business model and apply it to business areas outside our traditional memory architectures and chip-to-chip interfaces. Although traditional business wisdom says that the way to grow a company is by acquiring technology adjacencies, we aren't just doing that. We believe that the business model itself is the platform. Our focus is on understanding how to creatively invent and then creatively evolve our inventions into solutions. We see managing this activity as our core competency. We plan to continue our focus on technologies that fit into the company's overall mission: enriching the end-user's experience with electronic systems. Since the electronic systems market is quite broad, we believe we are well-positioned for technology and market diversification.

Philips has also struggled with the concept of invention versus innovation. Ruud Peters, CEO of IP&S explains:

There is a huge difference between invention and innovation. A patent merely protects an idea. We view innovation as the steps required to successfully create and bring a new product or service to the market. The creation and protection of an invention is a small and often early step in the total process. Although we are well-known for our research and breakthrough inventions and technologies, we have not always been able to transform them into successful products and services in the market place. In recent years we have learned to improve our success rate. Our company's current strategy is strongly focused on how we can create more meaningful innovations and bring them to the market faster.

Finally, Scott Frank, President and CEO at AT&T IP, has a different view of invention and innovation:

> AT&T believes that innovation and intellectual property are two of the major keys to its future success. We have traditionally used technology roadmaps to develop future products and services and protect them with intellectual property. To better ensure that we have identified as many good inventions and potential innovations as possible, over the last few years we have created and launched what we believe to be a state-of-the-art approach to capturing more creative ideas and creating even more valuable intellectual assets for AT&T. We call this new program The Innovation Pipeline (TIP).
>
> AT&T is filled with smart people, but for a variety of reasons, many do not participate in the development process for new products and services. Therefore, we decided to tap into the creativity of our employee base at large. We knew that individual employees often have kernels of useful ideas but don't think their idea is good enough or vetted enough to submit for our formal development process. Also, we knew that most employees don't know what the development process for a new idea is, or how to enter their idea into it. We have had a great patent program in place for years for employees to submit inventions that might eventually be patented, but the intellectual property team had never focused on getting these ideas commercially launched into the marketplace as successful innovations.

We worked within AT&T to develop a program that would reach out to all of our employees and encourage them to collaborate on ideas for products and services that could be commercialized in the marketplace. Employees were given a way to input their ideas, whether well thought out or not, through a user-friendly process. We decided to adopt the principles of social media, crowdsourcing, angel investing, and venture capital into our new program, TIP.

TIP consists of four phases. *Phase I: Social Invention* involves crowdsourcing. This social phase is conducted via an internal website where employees from any level, any organization, and any location can input their ideas. Other employees can collaborate through the site, and they can add to, comment, and vote on ideas. By asking our employees to engage in all of these processes we help the best ideas rise to the top.

The ideas that survive move to *Phase II: Pitch*. At the end of every quarter, we create presentations for the top ideas and pitch them to our internal *angel investors*, taken from the term used in Silicon Valley. The angel inventors are some of the company's top executives, including the Chief Technology Officer and Chief Marketing Officers from key business units. Each idea is given fifteen to twenty minutes to impress the angels, who then decide which ideas are worthy of investment.

In *Phase III: Project*, the originator of the idea has three to six months to bring their pitch to life. Often the originator does not have all the background required, so he or she is matched with a team to help build the idea into a prototype and construct a business case for it. Team members may be consultants, employees from our labs, or people with other skills.

In *Phase IV: Launch*, at the end of the three to six month time period the prototype is taken to a group of internal *venture capitalists*, many of whom are also angels. Venture capitalists recognize that they are investing their own organization's funds into the project. They examine each prototype and business case to see if it has what it takes to be impactful on their business. If venture capitalists actually fund an idea, it means that they will use it in their business unit's technology development roadmap and build it out. Ultimately, the idea, which became an invention, will now become a new product or service innovation in the marketplace.

At AT&T we differentiate between invention and innovation. Many IP management organizations in companies search their company for inventions and then protect them with patents. That process can create valuable defensive assets. However, most IP management organizations are not trying to ensure that those inventions are actually implemented and brought to the marketplace. Getting an idea into the marketplace is innovation and that means making money from the company's inventions. With TIP, AT&T Intellectual Property turns great ideas into potential inventions and ultimately into commercially successful product and service innovations.

The important thing to remember here is that company executives should discuss honestly where their company sits on the invention versus innovation spectrum. This conversation will provide clarity around what the true intangible core competencies are. Once that is known, then the conversation can progress toward discussing either monetizing invention or technology, or alternatively looking at implementing open innovation or something else within the spectrum. What we know is that company R&D budgets are under more and more scrutiny and it is unlikely that they will be able to cover all of the invention and innovation needs of the company in the future.

Best Practice 2: Managing IP Risk/Reward Trade-Offs

For companies at Level Four, IP is a strategic element of their business. For many Level Four companies, the CIPO has two primary objectives. The first is to maximize the value of the company's IP to its business; the second is to mitigate the risks associated with ownership of patents.

Managing IP Risk Many business managers find it much easier to understand and quantify the reward aspect of the equation, but need help in both understanding IP risks and quantifying them so that executives can make an informed business decision. This of course begs the question, "What are the IP related risks"? Let's focus on patents first. There are three main types of patent-related risks:

1. Innovation risks.
2. Intrinsic patent risks.
3. Environmental patent risks.

Let's look at each kind of risk more closely. To begin, innovation risk is the general risk associated with introducing a new product, process, or service. We discuss this and the other risks in the following sections.

Innovation Risk One common risk associated with IP is the risk of the innovation itself—the uncertainty associated with the introduction of a new product, process, or service. Examples of the elements of innovation risk are:

- **Technology Risk:** Will the technology ultimately perform as well as expected?
  - **Alternative/Disruptive Technology Risk:** Will competitive commercial alternatives emerge? Will disruptive technology eliminate the need for the solution altogether?
- **Adoption Risk:** Even if it works, will it be accepted in the marketplace?
- **Execution Risk:** Will the company be able to be successful in its innovation activities? Will it be able to commercialize the technology?
- **Market Risk:** If there is no current market for the technology, will a market evolve?
- **Infringement Risk:** Will the technology be covered by one or more third-party patents?

Environmental Patent Risk Another common type of patent risk involves the external environment—the risk that an external entity will change the rules of the system in a manner that will negatively impact patents. Types of environmental patent risks include:

- **Judicial Risk:** Will a new court decision affect our patents?
- **Legislative Risk:** Will a new law affect our patents?
- **Regulatory Risk:** Will a new regulation affect our patents?

Intrinsic Patent Risk   Finally, there are risks associated with the patent itself. Such intrinsic patent risks include:

- **Validity Risk:** Will previously unknown prior art surface that anticipates the patented invention or renders it obvious?
- **Enforceability Risk:** Will a prosecution issue result in an inability to enforce the patent?
- **Scope Risk:** Will a court construe the claims narrowly or broadly?
- **Design-Around Risk:** Will competitors find a way to create commercial substitutes that avoid the claims?

Gene Potkay, Chief IP Officer at Nielsen Systems, relates when it was that he knew he had succeeded in convincing company executives about the importance of IP and the risks associated with not having adequate protection for a product:

> Recently Nielsen was readying itself for a major product launch announcement. It was Sunday evening and the launch was scheduled for the next day. The marketing people had already prepared a product announcement for *Ad Week*. I was in the office and on the telephone with the marketing folks, outside counsel, executives, and the inventors. We were all engaged late into the night to ensure that we would first file for patent protection before any announcement would be made. Shortly before the meeting a very high-level executive announced, "We're not going to launch until we've filed for patent protection." And with that we held up the launch and moved heaven and earth until the patent could be filed.
>
> Holding up a major project launch announcement had never happened in my experience. Wow! Let me tell you, Nielsen is now very aware of the legal risk associated with launching a product before filing for patent protection!

It is often difficult for business people to understand intrinsic patent risks. From the businessman's perspective, an issued patent seems like it ought to be valid and enforceable. Sadly, however, that is not necessarily the case, as Percipience's Ron Laurie explains:

Patents carry two primary kinds intrinsic legal risk: validity risk and infringement risk. Let's look first at validity risk.

Patent validity is first and foremost a question of whether the most relevant prior art was: (a) *found*; and (b) *understood*, by the patent and trademark office (PTO) that issued the patent. This may be tested in court or (in the United States) in a post-grant review by the United States Patent & Trademark Office (USPTO), usually in the form of a reexamination proceeding. At the time of this writing, the criteria for assessing validity used by the courts are not the same as those used by the USPTO. Because of a statutory presumption of validity, the applicable evidentiary standard in court (which has recently been upheld by the U.S. Supreme Court) is that a party challenging the validity of a patent has the burden of demonstrating that the patent is not valid, i.e., that it should not have been granted, by "clear and convincing" evidence. The USPTO, however, is not bound by the statutory presumption of validity and thus does not apply such a stringent standard in a reexamination proceeding.

Turning to infringement risk, one finds that there are two sub-elements. The first is the risk or uncertainty associated with the scope (i.e., breadth of coverage) of the patent claims, and the second is the applicability of the claims as properly construed, to the products or services alleged to be infringing. Claims scope risk is typically resolved in the claims construction (or Markman) pre-trial phase of patent litigation. After the trial judge has determined the scope of the claims, infringement risk is then resolved by summary judgment if there are no factual issues, or at trial by the judge or jury. Of course, the determination of claims scope by the judge and the determination of infringement by the judge or jury are both subject to being reversed on appeal.

IP managers in Level Four operating companies are managing their firm's intellectual property with the above risks in mind. The following company discussions reveal how several of the ICM Gathering Level Four companies are managing to mitigate patent risk. Specifically discussed is how they are managing the following three elements of the risk management environment:

1. Quantifying the legal risk from Non-practicing Entities (NPEs).
2. New product IP risk.
3. Understanding legal risk.

Scott Coonan of Juniper Networks talks about how his company has been quantifying the legal risk associated with potential confrontations from NPEs:

> At Juniper Networks we've developed a framework for quantifying NPE risks. We engage in three different analyses. The first analysis examines the company's potential exposure by weighting exposure based on validity of the claims, the probability of assertion, and the probability of infringement. This is a coarse analysis where you estimate the revenues affected by the patent, and the probability of winning (or losing) at litigation, and then determine the net present value of the resulting product of those factors. That number is a rough estimate of the costs of litigation. We use that number as a baseline to determine whether it is possible to settle a dispute for less than that.
>
> The second analysis we conduct involves estimating what a lawsuit would cost even if we were to win. In this case we estimate the out-of-pocket costs for litigation, whether we were to win or lose. In this second analysis we estimate the amount of attorney fees and other litigation expenses to determine how much it would cost the company even if we were to prevail.
>
> There's a third kind of analysis that we pursue, using historical data. We've had enough of a history of defending and settling these cases that we now have our own data. We can compare a new or potential litigation against previous ones. This has proven particularly helpful for Juniper. We've been able to settle cases for quite a bit less than the amount suggested by either of the previous two analyses. As a result, when a new potential lawsuit presents itself, we look at it and say, "How does this compare to the other ones we settled for $50,000 or $100,000?" and use that as our measuring stick to stay within our own standards.

For Seungho Ahn at Samsung, the IP risk/reward trade-off is slightly different. "As an innovation and market leader Samsung is under immense pressure to find new markets and technologies, both faster and with less IP risk than before. So the IP group and our Open Innovation Group are working closely together to spot emerging trends and markets and to move quickly. When we were just followers it was easy because we knew the path. It is much more difficult to lead the industry and create the path."

A Juniper Networks Case Study on Litigation, as told by Allen Lo, Vice President of Intellectual Property, and Scott Coonan, Senior Director of IP Litigation and Patents

In December of 2001, Juniper Networks was contacted by Toshiba to take a license to a number of Toshiba's patents. In evaluating the assertion, we learned that their patents involved an older technology that didn't apply to our products. Toshiba and their attorneys, however, had a different view. Toshiba believed that, although their patents were initially directed to older technology, the more modern technology used in Juniper's router products incorporated that older technology and therefore Toshiba's patents covered Juniper's router products. At that time, Juniper's router business represented nearly 100 percent of Juniper's revenue.

In the end, we didn't feel that we should pay fees for a license we didn't think we needed. We were also influenced by Toshiba's litigation history. At that time the company had a reputation for not initiating patent lawsuits. Not surprisingly, we were not able to reach any agreement. In November 2003, almost two years after Toshiba initially contacted us about these patents, Toshiba sued Juniper in Delaware for patent infringement.

After some discovery, the first meeting to discuss potential settlement was scheduled for June 2005. Going into this meeting, we were concerned that the two companies' views

(Continued)

and interests were too divergent to reach settlement. On the one hand, we had no interest in paying any meaningful amount to settle a case we felt lacked merit. On the other hand, we were concerned Toshiba viewed this litigation as a one-time opportunity to generate licensing fees sufficient to justify the cumulative investment Toshiba had made over the years in building their patent portfolio, regardless of how valid their claims were in this case. Although we didn't know this definitively going into the meeting, we suspected that Juniper was targeted in part because Toshiba assessed Juniper's patent portfolio and didn't feel any risk that Juniper could bring a countersuit for patent infringement. After all, Toshiba is known for products such as consumer electronics, laptop computers, semiconductors, and medical imaging devices—products that Juniper's patents would not cover.

Our plan was to explain at the meeting how we believed the case would play out if we couldn't settle. Although we didn't feel we had a patent in our portfolio at that time that we could use to counterassert against Toshiba, we planned to acquire a patent and would file a suit against Toshiba targeting an area of higher exposure for Toshiba than Juniper's exposure. The meeting confirmed our concerns and suspicions, and neither company was persuaded by the other's position. So, not surprisingly, we didn't settle. In addition, Toshiba indicated during those discussions that they were not willing to attribute any value to a mere threat of a countersuit.

We examined our patent portfolio to see if there was something that we could use and found that we did not have countersuit ammunition in our portfolio because Toshiba was not doing business in our space (they were not a direct competitor). We also confirmed that most of our portfolio covered routing technologies and products. We then shifted our efforts to finding and acquiring from another company a patent that could be used against Toshiba and, indeed were able to find a company willing to let us acquire a patent that covered memory controllers, a technology applicable to Toshiba's laptop computers. We then sued Toshiba in a different jurisdiction and were successful.

From this situation we have learned a number of lessons that we have incorporated into our business.

- Toshiba didn't appear to think through the implications of their monetization desire. This was a perfect lesson on why you don't monetize without a clear strategy.
- Although one can't rely on this, it is sometimes the circumstance that the team on the other side makes mistakes that will be to your advantage. In the case of the Toshiba lawsuit, their litigation team made a number of tactical errors. Toshiba and its team pulled some discovery shenanigans for which they were severely sanctioned. This put them in a position where going into trial they had been sanctioned so badly they knew they had effectively lost already. In addition, they chose to assert patents on older technology and then creatively interpret the claims on those patents. Toshiba received an unfavorable Markman ruling in Delaware, and then decided to appeal the decision to the Federal Circuit. The last tactical error that proved helpful to our side occurred during the appeal, as Toshiba surprisingly refused to identify which were the critical claim constructions they were appealing. Although we believed we had a very sound case, it turned out that along with its strength, luck was also with us.
- We learned that if we get sued and don't have patent ammunition for a countersuit, we can still buy a needed patent.
- We also learned that it isn't just our competitors who may be the source of infringement lawsuits; it's anyone who has a patent that they think they can apply, and there are a lot of litigious noncompetitors out there.
- With NPEs, our philosophy is to demonstrate (especially to the law firms representing NPEs) that if you're thinking that Juniper would rather pay money than litigate a meritless or

(Continued)

weak assertion, you're wrong! We want to make such aggressors spend their time, effort, and money before they get anything from us, because if they want to make a decision about whether to litigate a weak case against Juniper, we would rather litigate than pay, no matter the difference between the two alternatives. Since establishing and following through on this stance, we've heard through the grapevine that some of the plaintiffs' attorneys who initially viewed us as a potential target decided not to sue for this very reason.

- Many NPE cases have multiple defendants and we get to see how close the other defendants' strategies are to ours. And without picking on any company or any firm in particular, we know that various companies have different tiers of representation; they have an A team, they have a B team, and they sometimes even have a C team. They make the mistake, we think, of coming to the fight, in these NPE cases, with the B or the C team, thinking that it is some kind of nuisance case. When they make that determination up front, they don't really know how difficult these cases may be, so they bring the B team and then the suit doesn't settle quickly. We've learned that smart plaintiffs target potential defendants who will be the easiest to defeat, and at Juniper, we work at not being such a potential defendant. Our legal counsel are attorneys who try lots of cases, so asserters know immediately that Juniper's going to be ready for trial. Every potential lawsuit is not the same and you may not need to spend all the money in the world defending each case to the death. But don't have a B team; instead have a B case strategy that may involve a leaner team. But bring the same folks to the fight.

Summary

Journeying forward with Thomas Edison, we've learned how Level Four companies use invention and innovation to their advantage and how they manage the risk associated with patent portfolios. This is knowledge that builds upon how companies create strong IP management functions at the Defend Position level, the Manage Costs level, and the Value Capture level.

Are you ready for the final and perhaps most exciting level of all—Level Five, where companies use their IP and other intangibles to Shape the Future?

Chapter 7

Level Five: Shape the Future

C ompanies that have achieved Level Five have come to understand the highest level of use for their IP as well as for their other intangibles. They look beyond defense, costs, and profits to focus on how IP can be used to shape the future of their company. At this level, the firm's IP and other intangibles are important tools to use in molding a desired future for the company. IP becomes more than a strategic asset, it becomes an enabling one. Companies at Level Five realize that their future can be defined within a limited set of parameters, and that progress toward that defined future can be managed (see Figure 7.1).

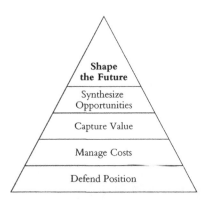

Figure 7.1   Level Five of the Value Hierarchy

What Level Five Companies Are Trying to Accomplish

Companies at Level Five view their IP from a perspective different from that found at the lower levels. At Level Five, company IP management objectives include:

1. Managing granted IP as business assets from which value of some kind must be realized.
2. Using patent applications as "technology option" investments to place bets and hedges on alternative business and technology futures.
3. Continually refining and updating the IP strategy and portfolio of patents and patent applications against the changing business and technology conditions.
4. Defining and influencing one or more desired futures.

Companies at Level Five understand three things about the future. First, the future is not knowable with any degree of certainty. Second, although the future is not knowable, a company can define several viable and desirable alternative futures for itself, and then work toward making one of them happen. This second point highlights our belief that it is possible to enable your company's desired future to come true. And finally, the object of defining one or more alternative futures from a company perspective is to be "in" one of these futures.

There are a number of ways to shape the future through IP, and the processes followed will differ from one company to the next. This chapter focuses on basic principles about the future and its context, and provides examples of how companies apply the principles, each in its own way.

In the first edition of *Edison in the Boardroom*, Level Five was defined as "Visionary" and highlighted best practices for the most sophisticated companies. In this updated edition, Level Five is also future-oriented but has evolved into a more proactive effort that looks into the future for IP and helps to shape the company future through IP.

The Characteristics of the Future

If a corporation's main objective for the long-term future is to exist profitably, then one of its main goals is corporate sustainability. When we wrote *Einstein in the Boardroom* in 2006, we dedicated an entire chapter to the importance of corporate sustainability and intangibles. In writing about IP's impact on corporate futures, we revisited our earlier work to see if there was anything we could utilize. In fact, there were quite a number of items. For example, what does corporate sustainability mean? *Forbes* magazine, in its 2002 Worldwide edition, used this definition: "Corporate sustainability is the umbrella for an expanding set of largely stakeholder-oriented challenges touching key aspects of business performance, competitiveness, and even survival."

The Gathering perceives corporate sustainability in two ways. Sustainability with a capital *S* describes how the firm acts or interacts with its community and with society on a long-term basis. But Sustainability with a capital *S* is not our primary interest here. Sustainability as it relates to this chapter is thought of with a small *s*. For IP management, sustainability is concerned with how the firm's current decisions affect its future value potential.

The Characteristics of Sustainable Corporations

Sustainability for business organizations does not mean preservation or permanence; rather, sustainability for businesses must be thought of in terms of adaptability, flexibility, and persistence; some even describe sustainability as organizational Darwinism. Sustainable corporations have a number of characteristics in common. For example, sustainable corporations:

- *Manage themselves for continuous economic growth.* This dimension of management activity has two very strong elements. First, the sustainable corporation manages itself internally so as to improve and enhance its innovation and productivity continually. On the external front, sustainable corporations constantly review and seek to enhance their market relevance as well as their relevance and importance to the firm's external shareholders.
- *Control and influence their destiny.* Sustainable firms recognize that they have the ability to control their own futures and exhibit a willingness to do so. These firms are quick to adapt to changes in their external environment. They have a culture of organizational change and a willingness to depart from the familiar. Their organizations lack complacency and exhibit a drive for continual renewal. They demonstrate a corporate capability for foresight and an ability as required to create their own future.
- *Demonstrate a sense of longevity.* Sustainable firms focus on dynamism and movement, not on preservation. Their view of the future extends beyond the life cycle of their key products or important technologies.
- *Have strong core values that are aligned.* Sustainable firms imbue themselves with values that are focused in the long term, values that are reflected in how the firm acts and reacts with its customers, its suppliers, its employees, and its shareholders.

Determining the Context of the Future

Context is the word we use to describe the multifaceted environment surrounding a future, event, or activity. We used it earlier in this book when we talked about the revenue streams an IP manager may generate from IP. The context of a revenue stream includes not only the specific IP at issue, but also the owner's intended use of the IP, the complementary business assets involved, the intended markets and customers, and the vehicle(s) for capturing the intended value.

Here, when we speak about defining the context of the future, we mean to define all of the important conditions that are associated with the future we wish to explore.

One such condition is the degree of precision needed to project the future. This can vary from one circumstance to another. For example, if an energy company is developing new power generation technology, the planning requires a detailed level of knowledge about the future (population center growths, power consumption per capita, permits, power transmission needs, etc). But if an IP manager wants to know whether a particular patent will still be important in 10 years, he or she may not find it necessary to project the future with as much technical precision.

For most business purposes, a moderately precise context for the future is sufficient.

So, what are the boundary conditions that may define the context for a business or an IP future?

One of these might be the degree of turbulence to be expected in the business or IP ecosystem. Igor Ansoff, considered by many to be one of the grandfathers of the strategic management movement, wrote about the challenges managers would face at the turn of the century. Ansoff suggested that in order to optimize a firm's competitiveness and profitability, it has to match its strategy and supporting capabilities to the firm's expected future environment. He suggested that there are five levels of turbulence in the business environments within which businesses reside. He recommends that companies match their strategic aggressiveness and organizational responses to the level of environmental turbulence they expect to experience in their company's future (see Table 7.1).

The first row of Ansoff's exhibit (moving from left to right in Table 7.1) shows five increasing levels of turbulence in the business environment and, for each level of turbulence, the different types of environments that organizations and managers will encounter. The second row in the table identifies the level of strategic aggression that is appropriate for each level, and suggests an appropriate strategic approach for the organization and its management. The third row in Ansoff's table highlights the organization's likely responsiveness to change and the types of changes the organization should seek.

The ICM Gathering members have come to recognize that they are now at Ansoff's highest level of a business environment turbulence. The

Table 7.1 Matching Turbulence, Aggressiveness, and Responses

Environmental turbulence	Repetitive Repetitive	Expanding Slow incremental	Changing Fast incremental	Discontinuous Discontinuous Predictable	Surpriseful Discontinuous Unpredictable
Strategic aggressiveness	Stable Stable, based on precedents	Reactive Incremental, based on experience	Anticipatory Incremental, based on extrapolation	Entrepreneurial Discontinuous New, based on observable opportunities	Creative Discontinuous Novel, based on creativity
Organizational responsiveness	Stability Seeking Rejects change	Efficiency-Driven Adapts to change	Market-Driven Seeks familiar change	Environmentally Driven Seeks related change	Environmentally Creative Seeks novel change

Gathering noticed this phenomena by looking backward at the nature of its discussions over the past several years. Prior to that time, most of the meeting discussions were about mutual learning, new practices, and new methods for creating and capturing value from IP. Recently, however, most of the meeting discussion has been around new and unexpected threats, events, or changes in the IP environment that companies may need to become aware of and could anticipate accordingly. In other words, the Gathering, by its very actions, recognizes that business has moved into Ansoff's most turbulent business environment, one characterized by events and threats that are discontinuous and unpredictable.

The importance of this observation is that IP managers and companies who are thinking about shaping their future must recognize that the context surrounding the future is *surpriseful*, characterized by discontinuous and unpredictable change. In the mathematical and financial communities, this instability of prediction is referred to as the "black swan."[1] In a recent article on the unpredictability of the future, the *Financial Times* noted, "Economic behavior is influenced by technologies and cultures, which evolve in ways that are certainly not random but that cannot be fully, or perhaps at all, described by the kinds of variables and equations with which economists are familiar. The future is radically uncertain and models, when employed, must be context specific."[2]

Success factors are another aspect of the context for the future of a business or its IP strategy. For companies interested in futures that are one year to four years away, these factors tend to focus on things the company must do to influence its immediate revenues or its expenses. For companies interested in futures that are five to eight years away, the factors tend to shift away from immediate income and expense activities to include economic, social, political, and economic issues that affect the entire industry. For companies whose future interest is beyond eight years, the parameters that affect company and IP success are almost entirely national, political, social, and economic factors (often called megatrends), that could affect the long-term viability of the business and its IP.

So, if an IP manager had conducted such an analysis, what would he or she be able to say in a description of the company's future context?

- The time span of the future period of interest would be defined.
- The degree of business turbulence and the firm's generally desired reactions to that turbulence could be described.
- The key success drivers for the company's business or for the success of the IP strategy would be noted and, for each parameter, the range of its potential states and stages could be estimated.

There are, of course, many other factors and bits of information one could use to further define the context of the future, but the list gives a representative set of parameters.

Note that the list does not describe a scenario; it describes a "window" of the future. It doesn't suggest that a specific set of parameters will describe the future. Rather it suggests that there is a range of the parameters that describe the context of the future. We don't know exactly where, within that range, the actual future will be, but we strongly suspect that it will be somewhere within the "column."

That, then, is how the authors see the context of the future.

Best Practices for Level Five: Shape the Future

Unlike the previous levels of the pyramid, Level Five companies are no longer looking only internally at how they can utilize IP; rather they are now focused outside the organization on how IP can help shape or change the dynamics of a market or industry. In addition, the time frames have lengthened considerably, often looking 5 to 10 years into the future. Given companies' needs to shape the future, Gathering companies have identified two best practices that are useful here; they are:

Best Practice 1: Define the context of your company's future.
Best Practice 2: Influence the future.

Best Practice 1: Define the Context of Your Company's Future

Defining the context of your company's future is not an easy task to accomplish; particularly in view of the many perspectives, internal as well as external, that could be taken into account. We suspect this very difficulty is a major reason why companies don't make more explicit efforts to define the future context for their company and how they expect to thrive within it. There is also quite likely a concern that to very openly discuss the company's future direction and strategies for influencing the future would be giving away too much information to current and/or future competitors.

Yes, it is possible to identify a desired future. It is particularly helpful, however, to make sure that that identification is consistent with the "envelope" within which the future is most likely to take place. Kevin Donnelly discusses how Rambus seeks to create its future:

> At Rambus, we focus on invention, on developing inventions into solutions (innovation), and on licensing both inventions and solutions to the market. We look for hard problems whose solutions will have a major impact on electronic systems. We believe this is a model that can work across technologies and markets. We have created a unique environment that fosters innovation and makes Rambus, as we like to say, "a company of inventors."
>
> Our development process is very much focused on defining the future. If system products represent a current generation and the semiconductor products in development are for the next generation, then people who are working on hard IP problems really have to be focused on the *next*-next generation. That forces a time frame that's literally many years ahead of today's market needs, and is much beyond what most businesses think about and invest in. It's hard to develop inventions for the future because, by definition, the future is uncertain. And although it's hard, it's something we have to be good at, because it is critical for our business.
>
> So, there are several things we try to do that might be useful or helpful for others to think about. The first is to openly and clearly talk about the time frames and the types of things we're trying to do and develop a culture where long-term thinking is part of our DNA. Rambus focuses on the longer-term, from our management and Board down through the organization (not just off in some lab somewhere), we try to encourage this long-term

thinking. Our management has made it clear to both the employees and our shareholders that Rambus has a long-term vision. You cannot focus on the future in quarterly installments.

In order to do work on what I call the next-next generation, you have to have a great understanding of the current generation and of the expectations for the next generation. At any given time, we'll have engineering engagements on products that are currently shipping. We also have development projects for the next generation, as well as lots of research on the next-next generation. Connecting those projects helps keep the future focus more grounded and more on target than if that work is done in separate divisions, separate facilities, or separate countries.

We're small, so we can't afford to innovate everywhere simultaneously. Of course, even the largest companies are resource-limited and can't afford to innovate everywhere. So you have to pick and choose the areas that you think are promising. We direct our research into areas of specific focus, and our choices are based in part on where we've had success in the past and, of course, where we believe we can have success in the future.

We do look at the so-called megatrends. What you really have to do is take that thinking to the next level and think about how those megatrends impact your key areas of focus, which in our case would be the systems of interest. We forecast what we believe will be the important high-volume systems of the future, and the anticipated requirements for those systems in the time frames of interest. We then brainstorm what hard problems will need to be solved in that time frame to meet those requirements. Technology trends are an additional input—for example, what is semiconductor lithography going to be like in 10 years—and we incorporate these trends into our research efforts. But even with our systematic approach to envisioning the future, we are not going to develop perfect solutions each and every time given such a long-term time horizon.

To deal with this inherent uncertainty, we seek to develop flexible solutions. By this I mean that we've invested a lot in solutions that can be adaptive or adjustable. Flexible solutions might have multiple modes to do different things depending upon how needs shift and what features actually become requirements in the future. That's a big part of our innovation strategy. Some of our most successful innovations have bridged the gaps between multiple and seemingly inconsistent types of requirements. We're able to accomplish this through what we believe to be very flexible solutions.

Ruud Peter of Philips describes the process IP&S uses to anticipate the future:

Each year we review the overall IP strategy with the board of management, and at a lower level we review specific IP strategies with the sectors and business units. As part of that review, we look five years into the future and beyond. Then, for each business, we determine:

- What is the competitive environment?
- How many competitors are in the market?
- What is the total market?
- How will this market develop?
- What is our market share?
- What is the ambition of the business?
- Do we want to grow our market share aggressively, or do we want to phase out?
- What are the supporting R&D programs?
- What is our technology position?
- What is our IP position compared with our competitors'?

Once the above information is collected, we determine what we call an IP value model—how can IP support the business in order to achieve overall value for the business? We then translate the IP value model into a financial model, and then we determine the IP portfolio needed to enable the company to realize the financial model. Once we know that, we look at the IP portfolio of today, determine the gaps between it and the IP portfolio we need, and decide how best to address those gaps. Can we do this by generating the required IP internally, funded by the Sectors,

Corporate, or IP&S? Do we need to acquire companies that have the technology together with the IP? Or should we just acquire the IP?

In this way, we end up with an IP strategy that is specific to each business and sometimes even for each product group within a business. Let's look at a real example of how this works. Philips is the number-one lighting company in the world, both in lamps and conventional lighting. As you may know, there's a complete revolution going on in the lighting business caused by the introduction of light-emitting diodes (LEDs). About eight years ago we looked at the lighting business and recognized that LEDs were going to become quite important to the market and told the business that they should focus there. At the time, the business people were too focused on their existing lighting business and were less interested in LEDs, as they weren't convinced that LEDs were going to impact the market on a large scale in the near term. Only after a strong push from IP&S and Research they changed course. We defined our goal as, "We want to become the number-one lighting company also in the LED business." We determined the technologies and IP that would be needed to achieve our objective. As a first step, we took a stake in a LED manufacturing company—Lumileds. Initially, we had a 50 percent stake and later we acquired the remaining 50 percent.

We also decided that we needed a strong position in LED controls and LED modules. We acquired Color Kinetics, a company with key technologies and a very good IP position. Their IP, along with the IP portfolio from Lumileds, together with the strong IP portfolio we had generated internally, created an LED lighting portfolio that we believe is the strongest in the world. We leverage that portfolio to facilitate faster growth of the LED market, thus enabling our own LED lighting business to grow quickly. We continue to add valuable IP to this portfolio and have made several more acquisitions in the field. A lesson we learned is that it is difficult to convince business management that their business will be severely impacted by disruptive technology. At IP&S we believe we always need to take the long-term perspective, whereas businesses frequently (and certainly in times of economic crisis) focus on the short-term to drive their business returns. We have learned that as an IP organization, you sometimes have to withstand the pressure from within the businesses and defend your position to best serve your customers.

At Procter & Gamble, the future is defined and shaped around one key focus: how to delight the consumer in both expected and unexpected ways. Steve Baggott explains how P&G interweaves its Open Innovation approach with consumer strategies to deliver the value, quality and market success to which it aspires:

Every P&G business unit has an innovation strategy that is reviewed with the CEO, the CTO, the CFO, and other key leaders. These reviews take place about once a year and include a full "soup-to-nuts" discussion of the strategic choices for each business. Those strategic choices then cascade into the innovation strategy, how resources are to be deployed, and priorities for Open Innovation.

How all that works behind the scenes is what turns strategy into effective action. Most of the businesses created an Open Innovation role in R&D, which we call a Connect + Develop Single Point of Contact or C+D SPOC. That individual often reports to the senior R&D leader for that business and facilitates Open Innovation work across that business unit (BU).

The people in these roles are key to P&G's Open Innovations work as they help formulate our search priorities, vet and screen external technology candidates, and build C+D awareness and expertise among their BU colleagues. For Bruce Brown, our current CTO, his goal is that Connect + Develop becomes a part of the way we all innovate, in all areas of the company.

Open Innovation is not something that you wake up one day and decide to do—"I'm going to start being external." It requires a balance of defined procedure and process, with openness to serendipity and unexpected opportunities, supported by the placement of the right people in the right roles.

Connect + Develop has truly been an innovation in how P&G innovates, and we will continue to drive collaborations that can benefit P&G and our partners.

In the first edition of *Edison*, the Visionary Level discussed using IP to change the nature and/or direction of your business or industry. Jim O'Shaughnessy of Percipience LLC has been an innovator in focused innovation, which was discussed in the first *Edison* edition. We checked back with him to see if he had any updates regarding his original thinking:

> Think about innovation workshops or complementary innovation as a gun that a CEO has in his holster, a gun that he knows will shoot. This realization quickly leads to the equally important question: Now that I know the gun will shoot, where do I aim it? *Opportunity Foresight* is a method I use in my consulting practice to help companies determine what kinds of innovation they can pursue, innovation that will put them ahead of their competitors within a short period of time.
>
> Opportunity Foresight is a process that allows one to gain critical insights or foresights about future opportunities. The magic of opportunity foresight is that it is used to create a context about possible paths the future may take. The object of the first step in the process is to create three equally desirable, yet mutually exclusive, contexts for the future.
>
> These contexts become important in several ways. They include telltales, named for the small flags on sailboat rigging that allows sailors to see the direction of the wind. Telltales may be thought of as small signs that a new trend may be about to occur. A lot of times, a trend emerges and you'll see it and say "Boy I should have seen that coming." The truth is, you're right! All the signals were there, but they were buried in a lot of noise. There wasn't a context to determine which signals were important indicators of the emerging future. Using our three contexts helps us to pick out signal from noise.
>
> Defining three possible futures, and the telltales for each, is invaluable stage setting as we begin the two other very important

processes. The first is to patent all around each of the technology and business opportunities suggested by each of the three potential futures. Creating target patents is done through complementary workshops, as discussed in the first edition of *Edison*. As the company begins to create patents for each of the potential futures it has identified, it closely monitors the telltales, and as the present unfolds, it can begin to see which of the potential futures is gaining the most traction. The company can refine its patenting program in accordance with the emergence of more and more information about the future that is evolving into place. The Opportunity Foresight process allows technology-based companies to make educated estimates of the patented inventions they will need to improve their competitive advantage position for the future.

Best Practice 2: Influence the Future

Over 30 years ago, professor, author, and consultant Stan Davis developed the concept of *beforemath*. "Many people," he said, "wait for events to happen and then they react or respond to them. When this occurs, people must deal with the aftermath of the event. But suppose things were turned around. Suppose you decided what it was that you wanted to occur in the future. If you made such a decision, and could visualize in your mind's eye what that future looked like, then you could manage the events between your present and that desired future . . . you would decide on the future you wanted to take place, and then deal with the beforemath of making it happen."

Some companies will choose a future that is well within the likely boundaries of their future context. In this case, the company now has created a new long-term objective, and can determine the activities and capabilities necessary to move the company from its current state toward the desired future.

Other companies, however, may identify a desired future that lies outside of one or more of their likely contextual boundaries. When this is the case, that company needs to identify the parameters that must be "moved" in order to allow the desired future to fall within their boundaries.

What we have found is that once a desired future is identified, companies have several options about how they can influence their business, industry, or eco-system to adopt positions, concerns, markets, standards, or products that are most beneficial to that future. They can exert influence by acting on their own behalf or with others. Most companies are very adept at identifying telltale signs that they can then exert influence by themselves to help achieve a desired future. Often such influences may include:

- Strategic alliances.
- Joint ventures or other collaborations.
- Marketing.
- Public relations.
- Lobbying.
- Litigation.

And indeed, within the IP space any and all of the above have occurred over the past 10 years. What is somewhat new, however, is the idea of cooperating with other companies to influence a collective future. To accomplish this, companies must work together to influence a desired outcome. Over the past 10 years we have seen companies cooperating to influence common IP outcomes such as RPX Corporation, Allied Security Trust (AST), or Open Invention Network (OIN). None of these initiatives, however, has brought about systemic change.

Ruud Peters, CEO of IP&S at Philips, describes how Philips thinks about the trade-off between what it does by itself and how it works with other companies:

> In determining new areas to invest in research for future business generation, IP&S provides guidance regarding the IP landscape to see whether it will allow us to conduct the future business the way we have in mind or if there are roadblocks in place. We identify potential partners already active in the same field, or highlight key IP to acquire or license to operate the business in the future.
>
> In this time of converging technologies, Philips does not have the money to develop all of the IP and technologies it needs for its future products. Even if we could afford it, we would lose

valuable time to market. Therefore we have to make choices about what we do ourselves, what we do in open-innovation collaborations with third parties, and what technologies and IP we acquire from the market.

We collaborate with other companies in many different ways, sometimes with two companies, sometimes with more than 80. Our collaborations can be at the early end of the technology spectrum, where we work with another company or university on an emerging new technology, but can also involve collaborating around specific products or markets. And of course, we work with others on establishing technology standards.

We believe in IP as a key driver for stimulating people and companies to take financial risks to invest in research and development with the aim of creating a new business, new jobs, and contributions to welfare in society at large. In support of that, we need well-functioning IP systems around the globe. We are actively contributing to creating an IP environment that we feel will adequately support our business interests. We do that directly ourselves, or through bodies or associations of which we are a member. We have a group of professional representatives in bodies and associations in all regions of the world, where they monitor any development in the law, regulation, standards, or any other areas that may have an impact on Philips' businesses. We determine whether or not we want to take any action and whether we want do that directly as Philips, in cooperation with other companies with similar interests, or through the bodies and associations in which we participate.

For the past several years we have found the ICM Gathering to be more interested in looking three to five years into the future trying to understand what IP issues were likely to occur so that they could then prepare their management and internal processes to handle the anticipated future. From this we have identified a list of nine systemic IP issues that should be considered underlying assumptions for the future. While the examples below are for the United States, each country will have its own list. Furthermore, by no means is this an exhaustive list.

1. There is an increasing amount of complexity around IP and IPM.
2. There is an increasing amount of technology convergence (e.g., handsets), which is creating new, sophisticated IP competitors.
3. This increasing convergence may make owning all of the IP necessary to enable your company's strategic objectives no longer possible or, at best, highly unlikely.
4. Companies may no longer be able to afford all of the R&D costs necessary to maintain and control their competitive advantage.
5. The amount of IP risk that companies need to manage is ever increasing.
6. The legal environment is also increasing in complexity, at both the national and global levels. In particular, the lack of IP law harmonization adds additional IP risk to multinational companies.
7. Although IP has been deemed an asset class by financial investors, there is an underlying lack of transparency that allows for significant arbitrage in the IP ecosystem.
8. Neither the courts, economists, nor companies know how to fully value legal risk, and thus, it is often assumed away.
9. Often in mergers and acquisitions, IP matters are not brought to the table since the unknowns and uncertainties related to IP could stall or even stop the deal.

The ICM Gathering companies have spent time exploring the systemic issues listed here, and are also in the process of looking for how companies may join together to combat them. While the group does not yet have an answer, the process of asking the questions has in itself been an eye-opening one. For example, is it possible to fundamentally alter the IP legal system to make it more efficient and less costly, and to reduce the complexity of IP cases? How have other areas of the law accomplished this (e.g., asbestos)? Or what would it require to get the United States to have a defined innovation strategy, then to clearly relate invention and IP rights to that strategy, and then to determine the appropriate funding necessary to have a fully efficient and effective PTO system?

It is easy to be a follower, but it is difficult to be the leader. Companies at Level Five are looking to be leaders. The good news is that whoever is first gets to define the future for all who come later. The bad news is, we may not get the future we desire. For a select few companies, that risk is worth taking.

Summary

Visionary organizations like the ones described here truly carry on the Edison legacy, and so can you. As a leader or advisor working with a technology-rich company, it is your job to be sure that the company's shareholders reap the value of its investments in IP. The IP Value Hierarchy can help you determine how your company measures up with others, both within and outside your industry, and where on the Hierarchy the organization or business unit should be. The Hierarchy can then also give you a road map for how to get to where you'd really like to be. Remember that much of your company's value is related to its intangible assets. You are the person minding that store, so mind it as well as possible.

Few companies today have completely mastered Level Three, let alone Level Four. There may not yet be any that are completely satisfied that they have reached the ultimate peak of success: Level Five, the Shape the Future level. It is possible for a company to be performing at several different levels in this hierarchy simultaneously. The basic question is how a company views the purpose and utilizes its IP to achieve it. When a company is willing to take advantage of the opportunities offered through exploitation of its IP and make conscious decisions on its effective monetization, then the level of utilization rises. As a company reaches the highest level of utilization, its focus on IP has permeated the company and is now extending beyond the organization itself and into the future.

Chapter 8

What to Do When You're Not on the Pyramid

Many people reading the original edition of *Edison in the Boardroom* commented that their company was not sufficiently intellectual property (IP)-sophisticated to reach even the hierarchy's first level: Defensive. We call such companies IP-*indifferent*. These companies have decided (albeit often implicitly) that IP is not particularly important for them.

Over the subsequent years, companies below Level One have asked us to offer some thoughts about what their companies might do to move the organization onto at least the first pyramid level of IP management. For companies asking this question, we suggest they consider the following four questions:

1. How do I know whether my company is on the Edison Value Hierarchy?
2. Should my company even consider managing its IP in a manner consistent with that recommended by the Edison Value Hierarchy?
3. Is my company destroying value by not managing its IP?
4. What steps might I take to prepare my company for entry onto the Edison Hierarchy?

Is My Company on the Pyramid?

Some companies tell us they are confused about *whether* they are on the Edison pyramid. Eric Oliver, VP, Legal Affairs of Sezmi and a long-time ICM Gathering member suggests that there are five questions such companies should ask:

1. Does your company have a written description of the intellectual property function and/or a defined person with a designated responsibility for intellectual property?
2. Is there a defined IP strategy or executive agreement as to the strategy? This may take the form of a few short points at a very high level, defining why your company is getting patents, copyrights, or trademarks. What do you plan to do with the IP you create?
3. Does your company have its own, independent, inventory of its IP? "Independent" means that your company has its own inventory, and doesn't rely solely on the inventory that may be housed with any IP law firm(s) you have retained.
4. Is there a defined process for deciding how many and which patents to file?
5. Is the IP function explicitly budgeted? In other words, is the IP function being held to the same fiscal management standards as other parts of the organization? Does it have to justify what it spends? Does it have to participate in the budget process, or does it simply access a pool of money as needs arise?

A "no" answer to even one of these questions, believes Oliver, demonstrates the company is not sufficiently IP-aware to categorize itself at even Level One of the Edison Pyramid.

Is My Company a Candidate for the Edison Pyramid?

First of all, not every IP-owning company needs to be intently managing its intellectual property. There are a number of good reasons why companies holding intellectual property may not need to be on the Edison Pyramid. In general, one may divide such companies into two sets:

1. *Managing IP does not make sense for the company.* For companies in this set it is most often the case that intellectual property is not strategic.
   a. Companies involved with commodity products.
   b. Companies whose products or services are not differentiable.
   c. Companies in industries that are mature and also in "harvest" mode.
2. *Managing IP may make sense for the company.*

Companies describing themselves as firmly in the first set need to read no further. They are probably okay being IP-indifferent. Their circumstance does not appear to call for further action.

But, for companies recognizing that managing IP may make some sense, they should consider a self-examination of the relationship between their business and the possibilities IP may offer. Only through such an exercise is it possible to determine whether managing the company's IP is sufficiently important to warrant an increased investment.

Self-Examination

It is often difficult for companies that are not sophisticated about the kinds of business value IP may provide to determine whether its value to them would be worth whatever kinds of cost they may have to incur to obtain it. After all, intellectual property is a business asset whose value often resides more in the future than in the present. Any process for arriving at an answer regarding whether a specific company should invest in intellectual property must inevitably look beyond the immediate or tactical situation and toward a longer-term perspective on the company and its objectives for the future.

Self-examination begins with an understanding of the company's business objectives. For example: a start-up company wishing to be bought by a larger company within a few years has very different needs for intellectual property than does a company with a long-term vision and objectives that include significant business growth over time. Companies in service businesses have different needs for IP than do companies engaged in manufacturing. Company size as well as corporate legal or tax structure may also affect the nature of an organization's need for IP. In short, there are no "cookie-cutter" answers as to whether or what kind of IP might suit a company best, but a reasonable self-examination is key to narrowing in on an answer.

For companies thinking about conducting a self-examination, there are several questions they may ask:

- How important are invention, innovation, and IP for your industry?
- How does your company's invention and innovation compare with your competition?
- How sophisticated is your industry about IP management practices?
- Could you obtain a significant competitive advantage over your competitors through the use of IP?
- Are there ways that IP could assist the company to achieve its business objectives? Which ones?
- Are there important ways IP could provide support to the company's business strategy?

The answers to these questions may illuminate an understanding of whether intellectual property is or should be important enough to your company to consider entry onto the Edison Value Hierarchy.

Characterizing IP-Indifferent Companies

For any company, it is imperative to become more aware of the ways in which intellectual property can provide support to your business. Increasing the company's self-awareness of intellectual property and its potential value can illuminate two things. First, it can help it understand why it has not placed value on IP; and second, it can lead to a self-examination of whether IP management is an activity in which the company should invest.

Companies that are IP-indifferent may be thought of as having a "blind spot" about intellectual property. By definition, a blind spot contains information about which the company is unaware. Companies on the Edison pyramid, however, know that it is to their advantage to minimize the size of the blind spot, and they take active steps to increase their self-awareness of intellectual property and its potential contributions to the firm's business.

For companies aware that they have a blind spot, but not aware of what it may contain, there are steps they can take to decrease the amount of unknown knowledge or information. Companies aware of their blind spot but who take no action to reduce its size are in jeopardy of being overtaken by an unpleasant surprise.

Examples of what may be included in a company's blind spot are:

- Abilities that are underestimated or untried through lack of opportunity, encouragement, confidence, or training.
- Fears or aversions about which the company is unaware.
- Unrecognized behaviors, attitudes, or company culture attributes that can be exploited by others.
- Unrecognized potential threats from outside the company.
- Unrecognized opportunities available to the company.

There are some examples of kinds of companies with a blind spot concerning intellectual property:

Companies That Are Poorly Informed about the Business Value of Intellectual Property

A number of companies hold the view that IP is something that lawyers take care of. They are entirely unaware of the commercial value of IP to their business. It has now been proven many times over that IP provides at least four very different sets of business value and, within each set, it may offer up to 20 or more specific kinds of value in support of a business. The four different sets of business value are: defensive, revenue-generation, cost-avoidance, and strategic or tactical positioning. Poorly informed companies are aware of intellectual property, but choose to not learn about its potential defensive and commercial applications to their business.

The Start-Up Company

Start-up companies are usually focused on achieving immediate business quantitative targets (e.g., sales). The company's entire orientation is toward short-term business objectives and it places enormous pressure on its officers to achieve them. In such situations, company managers, each desperate for more resources to help them reach their targets, argue against spending money on IP. The argument is that it won't help the company reach its immediate targets. If it won't help in the immediate run, and if our focus is the immediate, then why bother with paying for IP? Companies in this circumstance make a conscious decision to minimize their efforts to obtain and incorporate IP into their business. In other words, they willingly create an IP blind spot.

The Opportunistic Company

There are many companies whose business strategy is essentially to grab onto attractive opportunities as they arise and to exploit them to the fullest. Companies such as these live in the short run and usually have no credible vision of themselves in the future. They are usually managed by people having excellent exploitation skills but without a view beyond the next year's budget or the end-of-year bonus they anticipate. Such companies exist at the whim of industry or market trends and are usually not able to visualize either a desired future or the capabilities they must create in order to make that future a reality. These kinds of companies have a constantly shifting business focus. Because of this characteristic, they often believe that IP is a poor investment because their needs for protection and commercial support change in less time than it would take to generate useful intellectual property.

The Small Business

A small business may be thought of as anything from a one- or two-person company to a less than 50-person company. Although one tends to think of companies involved in retail activities, small businesses may be anything from industrial to technical to R&D or any of the many possible classifications of business specialty. Small businesses are usually characterized as unsophisticated, operated by people with a high degree of focus on their area of business specialty and lacking in the skills or capabilities associated with intellectual property. Although most small retail businesses have little need to be aware of intellectual property, many have learned that they have used a business name that is already claimed and protected by another entity. In most cases, small business problems with intellectual property may be avoided by a brief consultation with an attorney to create sufficient awareness about intellectual property issues, in order to avoid them.

The Culturally Bound Company

Some companies have grown (in some cases to become very large) without having acquired or used any intellectual property at all. Companies such as these argue that ". . . we have done well without it so far, why bother with it now?" Companies in this camp have no way of knowing whether and to what degree they may have destroyed or missed value opportunities and given away value to others. In some cases they have given away value to partners, customers, and suppliers by not recognizing the intangible value associated with the product, service, or exchange.

How Companies Can Destroy Value

Very often, companies destroy value they have created simply by not being aware of its worth to their own companies or to others. Harry Gwinnell, Vice President and Chief Intellectual Property Counsel at Cargill, suggests that there are nine possible ways that companies may be destroying business value for themselves through lack of management of their intellectual property.

1. *Lack of patents covering company invention or innovation.* Often an innovation can set new trends in the industry and, in some cases, establish new standards for the industry. With no IP protection, however, there is no opportunity to be compensated for such a contribution to the industry. Companies in this situation destroy value they have created by leaving money on the table.
2. *Lack of protection for trade secrets.* Many times one hears managers talk about "trade secrets" and their value to the company. But, when

asked about the steps being taken to protect them, one may be informed that there really isn't an active program for trade secret protection. By not taking active and appropriate steps, the company often ends up giving away some of its important commercial information—information that provides it with a competitive advantage, without being compensated for it. Also, the research dollars invested in those developments, without compensation, go right down the drain. This is a second example of destroying value by not receiving compensation.

3. *Not protecting the proprietary information of your customers or partners.* If a customer or partner gives you proprietary information—technical or business—relating to their products or processes, there is a natural expectation that you will protect that information. A failure to do so represents a clear breach of trust. It often takes years to build trust and, once lost, it is hard to rebuild. Your firm could easily lose business or licensing and partnering opportunities associated with that breach. And, depending on the size and publicity surrounding the breach, there could be competitive damage associated with the breach.

4. *Lack of an inventory of company intellectual property.* If the company doesn't know what intellectual property it has, how can it determine:

Whether it actually has the protection it believes it does?

Whether it has access to commercial opportunities that IP can provide?

Having a comprehensive inventory of the intellectual property the company owns can provide a real competitive advantage.

5. *Lack of a database that matches products and services to the company IP portfolio.* While mapping your intellectual property to the products and services it protects may seem like simple common sense, it is something that companies rarely do. But, by not knowing what IP relates to what products or services, companies can find themselves in the value destruction space. For example, companies may not be aware of opportunities for licensing by not knowing what kind of IP is available. When your company decides to sell a business, knowing which patents should be sold, and which ones you want to retain licenses to, which patents are already licensed, and so forth becomes a difficult task to complete. And, if time is limited (as it usually is)

the company can easily not get the full value of the IP it transfers with the sale, thus destroying value it has created over time.

6. *Retaining patents that don't relate to current or potential business.* Very often patents and other IP in the company portfolio, which might have been needed in the past, may no longer be useful to the company. Particularly in the case of patents, these generate costs, such as maintenance fees, which is value-destroying in this circumstance.

7. *Failure to monitor company IP agreements (especially licenses).* Companies sometimes learn, too late, that they have been paying licensing fees for use under patents that had since expired. In other cases, companies find they have licensed a patent to more than one party where an exclusive license had already been given. Or, money was received under company patents that had expired. Circumstances such as these indicate that there is value destruction going on in one form or another.

8. *Putting only cash into partnering arrangements.* When your company is approached for a partnership arrangement where the company's contribution is to be cash only, a red flag should be raised. In such cases, the other party may be putting in less money, or in some cases no money, because they are providing other contributions, such as other assets (both tangible or intangible, such as IP). Although it is possible that your company has been approached simply for funding, it is more likely that you bring something else "to the party" that makes you an attractive partner—whether it is marketing capability, technical know-how, international reach, and so forth. Discovering what these factors are provides your firm with more negotiating power and an opportunity to lower your cash input. The attractiveness of your company as a partner is typically based on what you have to offer, a gap that you fill for the other party. So, if all you are bringing to the deal is money, then you have two options:

   1. You were approached solely because you have available cash, which makes you "dumb" money.

   2. You have intangibles available, but are not aware of what they are. In this case, you would be giving them away, which also makes you "dumb" money.

9. *Under either option above, it is possible you may destroy company value without realizing what it was and how much it was worth.*

Moving toward the Edison Hierarchy

So how does an IP-indifferent company move itself toward the first level of the IP Value Hierarchy? Erik Oliver of Sezmi suggests that there are three steps a company must take. He uses a start-up company to illustrate his perspective.

There are three requirements companies must satisfy if they wish to create an IP function. The first involves finding someone to spearhead the function's creation and functioning. At the outset that person will most likely be an attorney. But, of greater importance, that person must have an interest in intellectual property and be able and willing to commandeer other resources to build an IP function. The major factor in selecting the person is that they must be interested, focused, and able to marshal resources to make the IP department function—an IP enthusiast. The second is that the IP enthusiast needs to be involved with defining the IP strategy, one of the requirements for moving toward Level One of the pyramid. The third is that the IP enthusiast must communicate regularly with management on IP issues with reports and well-defined metrics.

Employing Metrics

It is important that the IP enthusiast begin reporting to management about the company's early efforts. Those early reports may just be *quantity* metrics. Although measures of quantity are only a small part of an IP function's story, at the early stage of its development, just knowing that the company filed its first patent may in and of itself be a significant reporting event. More generally, however, the reporting and metrics should align with the company's three- to five-bullet strategy. If your strategy is "We are going to have a handful of patents so that five years now, we have some flexibility," then you want to demonstrate that you are working up to that point. At the outset, just count what can be counted.

Participating

The second requirement is that the IP enthusiast needs to "elbow" his or her way into the company's cadre of managers. Otherwise, he or she will be viewed as less than equal, and thus poorly positioned to effect change.

The IP enthusiast needs to develop processes for IP-creation that are appropriate for the company—processes targeted 12 to 24 months ahead. The IP enthusiast must come up with ground rules, methods for ranking, and some decision criteria that the company can use for the next 12 to 24 months. The processes will then evolve with the organization and its strategy. So, as the company's business strategy descends from a high level view in the form of a few sentences to a more refined and detailed strategy, the IP enthusiast is going to have to create more detailed processes that are appropriate for the people in the team.

Also, as soon as possible, the IP enthusiast should start participating in the company's planning and budgeting processes. Although the IP function's budget may be small, the IP enthusiast who is committed to participating on equal terms within the organization for budgetary resources is a crucial step. Setting that stake in the ground and making it clear that the IP function is going to participate as a budgeted activity is important.

Managing

The third requirement involves building some tools to assist with managing the company's intellectual property. Typically this involves mastering some existing, available tools, which can be as simple as an Excel spreadsheet or a low-cost prepackaged cloud-based solution. Creating simple and low-cost tools is an important step in learning about what kinds of management activity the IP function is really going to involve itself with, and what capabilities it needs to assist with that involvement. Buying an expensive off-the-shelf computer-docketing system with many capabilities, without knowing what capabilities are important to the company, is an often-deadly mistake.

Summary

Many companies are concerned that they don't appear to "qualify" as IP-savvy management participants in the Edison Value Hierarchy, even at its lowest level. Companies with this concern may ask themselves a series of questions to learn whether intellectual property is or should be sufficiently important to their business to warrant investing in IP management. For companies that are aware of the importance of IP to their business, but that question whether their IP activities meet the standard of "IP management," there is a further set of questions that may be asked. Companies not paying adequate attention to their proprietary and legally protected inventions may be destroying value that they have invested in creating. Examples are given of commonly found circumstances of value destruction by IP-indifferent companies. Finally, there is a set of recommendations that companies may follow to move themselves from a condition of inadequate IP management to a position where they may qualify for inclusion in Level One of the Edison Hierarchy of Value.

Chapter 9

The Procter & Gamble Journey

Innovation has been the lifeblood of the Procter & Gamble Company (P&G) throughout its nearly 175-year history. For most of that time, innovation was almost entirely done inside the company—ideas and technologies developed by scientists and researchers working to meet consumer needs. On occasion, P&G would selectively bring in assets from the outside, or do some equally selective joint work with strategic partners. But, in large part, P&G's innovation came from within.

And so it went, for generations. As is the case with many leading innovative companies, P&G developed more great ideas than it could use. With some, P&G learned the innovation wasn't as attractive to the company or consumers as first thought, or it proved to not be a strategic fit with P&G's business plans. As a result, P&G ended up with a sizable number of intellectual property (IP) assets that sat on the shelf. It was this realization that set P&G on a journey to reach out, to extend its IP to others, and to embrace open innovation as a key strategy to win.

Beyond Make and Sell

In the mid 1990s, a P&G vice president proposed that the company test a potential new revenue stream by licensing selected pieces of P&G's IP assets to external parties. Additionally, the company could direct that income stream back into additional innovation, which would give rise to more IP.

Leadership was intrigued and agreed to fund a small pilot team to test the idea. In the summer of 1996, the company appointed an experienced P&G vice president and general manager, Jeff Weedman, to head what was to be called "Global Licensing."

Weedman quickly built a team of about half a dozen people, understanding that they had only two or three years to prove that out-licensing could work for the company. The first key milestone was to generate more revenue than the team was costing in overhead. Next, Weedman knew they needed to generate a large enough income stream that out-licensing would become an attractive new business opportunity for P&G.

"It was an interesting proposition. But we faced some sizable hurdles right at the start," said Weedman.

First, the group was established as a profit center, meaning that any income the team generated by out-licensing a business unit's intellectual property would be credited to Global Licensing, not to the business unit holding the intellectual property. This made it difficult to sell the proposition to business units. "In essence, we were trying to convince them to let us sell their children off the back of the truck—and that Global Licensing would keep all of the money from the sale," Weedman said.

The second challenge: the new team didn't have any visible endorsement from company leadership. As a result, they went with hats in hand, trying to find people interested in taking P&G possessions and share them outside. It was a tough task.

Critically important in the group's early story of survival and success was that it was placed under the senior leadership of Steve Donovan, group vice president for P&G's Snacks and Beverage business at the time. Donovan believed in the project.

The group focused its early efforts on Donovan's beverage and snack business units. It was the head of beverage R&D who was one of the first to say he might have something of interest. It turned out to be calcium citrate malate, or CCM—a patented technology that developed into a pivotal and signature monetization effort for Global Licensing.

CCM was an innovation with tremendous potential. Through research in Oral Care and other business areas, P&G learned how to effectively work with calcium, and ultimately how to create a superior form of calcium that was more bio-available. P&G incorporated CCM into the orange juice product it then owned, introducing Citrus Hill Plus Calcium in 1986.

At the time, Citrus Hill was competing against Coca-Cola's Minute Maid business and Tropicana, and unfortunately, was not as successful as P&G had hoped. The company later bought the Sunny Delight juice drink business, for which it also offered a plus-calcium line extension. Yet this too proved to be a fairly small business opportunity. While the company believed in CCM, it decided to exit the orange juice business. Left behind were a number of calcium-related IP assets.

Out-Licensing Technology

P&G beverage leaders knew they were sitting on something important. CCM proved in clinical testing to reduce the risk of osteoporosis and fracture among postmenopausal women. The company had formulation expertise, an IP and patent position, and a very strong roster of clinical test results that would support claims that outside parties could make under license. Plus, it was ready to go—it could be easily incorporated into other formulations or products. And, consumers liked it because it did not have the white, chalky appearance and taste negatives of some other forms of calcium on the market in orange juice products at the time.

And so, CCM became Global Licensing's first licensing project. The team ultimately partnered with Tropicana, which successfully commercialized CCM, leveraging the technology and the claims from

P&G's clinical trials. When Tropicana was acquired by PepsiCo, the calcium story became integral to their efforts in juice as well.

But there is a part of the CCM story that doesn't relate at all to monetization; it relates to P&G's mission, which is "to touch and improve the lives of consumers around the world."

"For us, leaving on a shelf a technology that could potentially help improve the diets—and health—of millions of people, went against our core. It was something none of us was comfortable with," Weedman said.

By partnering with Tropicana, P&G was able to extract additional value and return for the company's shareholders and improve the lives of consumers.

Internally, the impact of the CCM project and Tropicana partnership was resounding. It moved Global Licensing from being a cost center to delivering bottom line incremental value. Across P&G, people could now see the value and potential of working externally and became much more interested in supporting the work of Global Licensing. Once it was demonstrated that licensing could be quite attractive, resources began to flow, and it became far easier for the group to penetrate other business units that might have different, richer, deeper, or broader patent opportunities.

"Looking back, there was one element in our early work that really opened the door and enabled our success. And that was identifying a champion within the Company to support our work. That proved much more valuable than even finding the golden technology to license," said Steve Baggott, an original member of the Global Licensing team and now Director of Global Business Development. "Lucky for us, our champion was also someone who was willing to take some smart risks."

Additional Growth via Effective Policy Changes

The success of the CCM project earned the Global Licensing group a right to play—at least for a while longer. They still needed to establish an ongoing portfolio of projects, though, and faced some serious challenges. First, they were continuing to collect revenue from IP that was owned by other business units. And while they were gaining internal champions, they still had not secured legitimization from top P&G leadership.

But in 1999, things began changing in the group's favor. First, the company streamlined and consolidated its financial reporting structure, which meant that the small unit would no longer be a profit center. Thus, any value the team brought in would now flow back to the owner of the intellectual property and/or whoever had contributed to the external commercialization of those assets.

The second change that helped the group was a policy statement from the CEO outlining a new patent policy that included a call to institutionalize out-licensing of intellectual property as a legitimate option for value creation. Specifically, the policy said that a business had exclusive patent rights for three years from first commercialization, or five years from when the patent was granted. If the business failed to develop commercial value within that time, the patent became fair game for other P&G units (such as Global Licensing) to seek other opportunities for monetization. The reasoning behind the policy change was simple. Durk Jager, P&G CEO at the time, was committed to licensing; he knew that P&G was using only about 10 to15 percent of its patents and that the potential to put them to good use externally was substantial. He also wanted to create internal competition to drive focus and excellence. He believed that if P&G's Research & Development teams knew that Global Licensing could take their innovations and sell them outside on the open market (including to competitors) in a relatively short period after they invented them, they'd be much more inclined to better focus on projects that had solid potential, strategic relevance, and business support.

With this very visible endorsement, Global Licensing's portfolio of work grew markedly. From there, the Global Licensing team began asking themselves and others in the company a very logical question: What other types of IP did the company have that might be mined for value? Like most companies, P&G essentially had two other types of IP: trademarks and know-how.

Reinventing and Integrating Trademarks and Brands

For P&G, their brands and trademark names have always been the crown jewels of the company. "Our brands make an ongoing promise that when consumers buy Tide or Pampers or Gillette, they also are buying a promise of quality and value," Baggott said. "The trust consumers give us is built up over decades of stewardship of those brands."

Thus, when Global Licensing started talking about expanding its work by sharing P&G trademarks with partners externally, the discussions were again not easy. But this time, Global Licensing had a bigger benefit in mind than just additional revenue generation—a benefit that in time appealed to even some of the company's most guarded brands. The proposal was that by licensing its name, a brand could quickly and efficiently expand its portfolio to reach more consumers in areas where P&G lacks either core expertise or manufacturing capability.

One of the group's first partners, and still one of the company's strongest stories, was with a then relatively-small but solid company called Kaz. Started by a father looking to provide comfort for his sick son, Kaz designed the world's first electric vaporizer. The company quietly grew into the leading vaporizer manufacturer in North America.

Meanwhile, P&G owned Vicks, the market leader in over-the-counter respiratory products. Vicks was looking to expand its offerings to reach more consumers. P&G connected with Kaz. It was a company rooted in quality, consumer service and innovation, and fit soundly with the Vicks equity. P&G signed a licensing deal with Kaz, putting the Vicks name on Kaz vaporizers and humidifiers. Neither company ever looked back.

Within just six months, the Vicks Vaporizer became the number one selling vaporizer in North America, and the category grew by more than 20 percent. The partnership has continued to grow, helping expand both Kaz and the Vicks business. Today, Kaz's Vicks Healthcare Products include more than 130 products, including vaporizers, humidifiers, dehumidifiers, and thermometers and are sold in 20 countries.

Continued innovation, marketing, co-marketing promotions, and strong retail presence have grown market shares to 80 percent in vaporizers, 60 percent in humidifiers, 32 percent in thermometers—all at least triple the next largest brand. In 2006, P&G extended its relationship when it sold its Braun thermometers and blood pressure monitoring devices to Kaz. Both the Braun and Vicks businesses have grown more than 25 percent.

Through this partnership, P&G was able to extend the Vicks brand into other very logical and strategic adjacencies that built the brand and delivered a more holistic solution to consumers under the Vicks brand. Kaz has grown as well, leveraging the trusted, household Vicks trademark to help grow its business and expand into new retailers and new markets.

For most of P&G's brands, which generate hundreds of millions or billions of dollars per year in sales, the licensing royalties are not generally going to make or break a particular business. Far more important is how the brands leverage the partnerships strategically to build and strengthen their products' equity.

Leveraging Internal Know-How

P&G's second area of opportunity for external partnership and value creation was know-how. For this, Global Licensing looked first to its manufacturing capabilities and a suite of software, manufacturing processes, and training tools that P&G has come to call Reliability Technology (RT). This program was originally developed in collaboration with Los Alamos National Labs (LANL). LANL modeled, developed, and tested the mathematical algorithms that are part of the foundational science of RT.

RT had for years enabled P&G to produce on-spec, high-quality products at a very reliable rate, greatly reducing cost and waste and increasing efficiency. With manufacturing operations all around the world, this proved to be a tremendous capability for P&G as they were able to get more products from their installed base, and thus could defer adding more manufacturing capacity, which is costly for any business. They also saw improvements in quality, which is a core value for P&G.

Knowing first-hand the value that RT could bring to a company, Weedman's team worked to package its strong set of proprietary tools, methods, and processes. In the early 2000s, they received agreement from leadership to explore monetizing P&G's RT knowledge and processes with other, non-competing companies. The team had some initial wins.

But capacity limited success. They learned quickly that sharing know-how demands a solid transfer of skills and knowledge, supported by training. Thus, expanding this program would require P&G taking a lot of its people away from working on P&G businesses—not a preferred solution—or creating a business-to-business P&G service division that could focus on monetizing know-how.

Weedman's team—now called Global Business Development—didn't like either solution. They determined they couldn't do it themselves, and began looking for an external partner. The ultimate fit was a collaborative partnership with Ernst & Young (E&Y). P&G brought the technological expertise and E&Y offered its well-established consultancy practice. Thus, P&G's RT product fit very nicely into E&Y's strategic direction to build out its supply chain advisory practice.

P&G has now trained a core E&Y team to become highly skilled in RT. Together, the two companies have developed RT Leadership Training, as creating a reliability culture within any organization challenges many of the existing manufacturing paradigms. The team has already licensed and deployed RT to a few Fortune 200 companies. E&Y is leveraging its strong base of consultants and practitioners to offer RT as an additional capability area to its clients, and P&G then shares in the return.

"While we are still building this new proprietary know-how–based business model, it already has shown tremendous promise," said Mark Peterson, Director, Global Business Development and leader on the RT project with E&Y. "We already have licensed RT to a small number of companies who are reporting really resounding results. This capability is driving significant cost savings for our clients within 12 to 18 months of deploying RT."

But there's another interesting aspect to the RT story. Taking RT outside actually made P&G stronger inside. When P&G began taking RT to other companies, they codified the technology so that it could be transferred to external parties, thus providing P&G teams with a much more robust and readily deployable set of tools for internal use. Plus, RT licensees gave feedback that strengthened the program still further. P&G trained 48 of its own plants on the improved RT program in just nine months. "This showed that we can improve our own know-how when we take it out and bring it back in, sharpening our own game," Peterson said.

Looking Externally

The fourth chapter of the P&G Open Innovation story is probably the most well told. It started in early 2000, when A.G. Lafley had just been named the company's new Chief Executive. He inherited a difficult business situation. P&G's stock price had suffered over the preceding few quarters after the company missed some of its targets. Lafley knew that there were a number of areas that needed sharper focus for the company to get back on track.

One notion was that the Company needed to be much more externally facing. He set the tone immediately when he did something no other P&G leader had done. He visited the P&G Alumni Association, a group of former employees who had either retired or left the company, with many going on to leadership roles in other companies and organizations. Historically, once someone left P&G, they were considered "out of the family." A.G. had a different point of view.

To him, everyone was a possible asset in helping grow the P&G business. And that included all employees—current or past. P&Gers, he said, are deeply loyal to the company, even after they've left. Who better to partner with? From those first days as CEO, Lafley began redirecting the company to become much more externally friendly.

He really made that vision take root when he announced that P&G would source 50 percent of its innovations from external partnerships. At the time, it was estimated that less than 10 percent of the company's innovation was fueled by external collaboration. "This was a stretching goal," Weedman said. "And none of us really knew how we'd get there." Lafley recognized that the pace of innovation was quickening. Competition was getting fiercer and faster. He knew that to stay in the forefront they would need to be even more effective innovators.

Open Innovation, he said, was a way to complement, augment, and accelerate what his teams could do internally. Additionally, enlisting talents outside the company would free P&G resources to focus more on those core areas where P&Gers could uniquely deliver.

He also wanted to ensure that partnering with P&G for innovation would be the most attractive option for external innovators and companies, and thus innovation would come to P&G first.

Under that direction and with that tone set, the company began the journey of Open Innovation, importantly led by R&D and the company's CTO. It was an approach they quickly branded as Connect + Develop (C+D).

As in P&G's earlier years with licensing, the company quickly saw that there were early adopters, those who needed more time to adjust, and everything in between.

Businesses to adopt early were typically somewhat leaner than others. They had lots of areas in which they wanted to innovate, but finite amounts of R&D resources. Bringing in external resources promised to be a big enabler.

One of the big early wins was in Home Care with Swiffer Dusters. P&G had recently launched the Swiffer brand, giving consumers a different and better way to clean. It also established what is now called the "quick clean" category, both defining and then delivering a whole new source of consumer delight, and a source of sales to P&G's retailers.

To expand into new products that might follow naturally from the original Swiffer floor cleaning cloth, P&G marketers and researchers turned to other cleaning tasks in the home. They learned that consumers were looking for a better way to get rid of dust elsewhere. That caused them to create an internal program to develop a dusting tool.

During the time the internal teams were working on a dusting solution, the R&D leader for Home Care was visiting his technical team in Kobe, Japan. He happened to see a product from Unicharm—a major Japanese consumer goods company—in an employee's office. The disposable duster product with a sleek plastic handle was a far better innovation than the one his team was working on back home. The question became, would P&G be willing to access the assets of Unicharm—a fierce competitor to P&G in Asia—in order to advance and accelerate its innovation program? And would Unicharm be interested in such an arrangement?

P&G eventually decided it was worth trying. They were able to structure a partnership that soundly benefited both them and Unicharm. P&G offered Unicharm the manufacturing, distribution, and marketing scale Unicharm did not have and that was needed to bring their innovation out of Japan and make it global. Today, Swiffer is one of P&G's 50 Leadership Brands, sold around the world.

Another story comes from P&G's Oral-B business. P&G Oral Care was looking for a strategic expansion of its dental-care line. A pulsating toothbrush was on the drawing board, but still had up to five years to go in development. Through C+D, the company found a Japanese firm with a product matching P&G's vision. The partnership, coupled with additional P&G R&D, resulted in the Oral-B Pulsonic Toothbrush. It launched in less than a year.

And then there was the company's joint venture with Clorox—another P&G competitor. This story began in 2003 when P&G researchers, working on diapers, developed technologies that would deliver superior non-tear and adhesive properties for plastic film. P&G teams quickly recognized a range of potential application for these innovations in the food wrap industry. But this was outside of P&G's strategic focus and existing manufacturing capabilities, so P&G developed a joint venture with Clorox, in which P&G's innovations eventually led to the creation of Force Flex trash bags and Press'n Seal food wrap. The partnership was a solid win for both companies—and for consumers. For Clorox, Glad sales doubled.

Innovation in partnership continues. Recently, P&G brought its Febreze technology to the Glad Joint Venture, resulting in the August 2010 launch of Glad Odor Shield with Febreze, which neutralizes trash odors. It was an immediate market success.

P&G has done a great deal of analysis on the power of its C+D initiatives. The company has seen C+D projects deliver about 70 percent greater value than initiatives that were not powered by Open Innovation. That is because through C+D, teams can often accelerate the "time to money," which tends to improve the net present value of the project. It may also reduce the amount of the company's upfront investment in R&D resources.

P&G's perspective on C+D has evolved as its teams have worked with the concept now for several years. They now think of it as including two different types of open innovation. One is the strategic and highly directed proactive C+D, and the other is serendipitous, often reactive, C+D. (We discuss these in Chapter 6.)

As the company moves forward, C+D's goals are to support business units and corporate functions on strategically identified and directed needs, and to strengthen external searching. The latter ensures that the company has the first look at outside innovations that could be relevant and applicable to the business.

What exactly is P&G looking for in these searches? It runs the gamut. For one, P&G looks for cooked products, something like Swiffer Dusters that are either already on the market or ready to market. This includes IP or a proprietary position, and a pipeline of future improvements. Cooked products are downstream ideas.

P&G also looks for innovations that are far upstream, such as a particular molecule that would feed into a long-term development program, enhancing and strengthening work already underway. Sometimes search results give rise to joint development agreements where P&G will work collaboratively with the outside party. In other cases, the company may simply need to access a partner's IP, and then continue development on their own.

Clearly, IP and other intangibles are very important. P&G looks for those intangibles—whether it's know-how, patent protection, or some other sort of capability—where it can have a proprietary position. The consumer goods business is fast-moving and competitive. The ability to have and sustain a proprietary position has proven time and again to be a core element of P&G's business model.

IP as an Enabler to Innovation

So how does this all link up inside P&G? As this has proven to be key in enabling the work of Open Innovation, it's valuable to look quickly at the structure that supports the work.

Every P&G business unit has a business strategy and an innovation strategy. These are reviewed annually with the CEO, the CTO, the CFO, and others in leadership. Their strategic choices are identified, as well as how they cascade into the innovation strategy and the innovation program and how resources are being deployed.

Across R&D, P&G also has embedded experts who report to the senior R&D leadership and facilitate Open Innovation work for their particular business. That person is a key partner for Open Innovation work. They help Global Business Development teams formulate search priorities, vet, screen and talk with outside partner candidates, and generally facilitate Open Innovation awareness and training across their business areas.

As a general rule, P&G does not seek an IP or proprietary position on things that the company doesn't envision commercializing.

This was a key strategic choice for P&G. "Even if we come across an innovation that everyone really likes, we take a long hard look at how it fits with our business strategies. If it does not support or advance where we need our business to go, then we pass," Weedman said. "We do not try to capture it or the IP simply because we either like it, or don't want someone else to have it. In fact, if it's not a fit for us, we very often will try to connect the innovator with someone else—even if it's a competitor. We're not looking to stand in the way of good ideas reaching the consumer, we just want to see them first, and have the first chance at delivering the biggest win for us, our partner and the consumer."

Looking Forward

As P&G looks toward the future, it aims for Open Innovation to play an ever growing role in accelerating innovation and delivering value to its consumers. In fact, the company's current Chairman and CEO, Bob McDonald, has taken Lafley's C+D goal to a new level.

He is calling for C+D to triple its contribution to P&G innovation by delivering $3 billion toward the company's annual sales growth through Open Innovation. He also is calling for P&G to be recognized as the Partner of Choice for innovation partnerships.

"Connect + Develop has created a culture of open innovation that has already generated sustainable growth; but we know we can do more," McDonald said when he announced the new goals in October 2010. "We want the best minds in the world to work with us to create big ideas that can touch and improve the lives of more consumers, in more parts of the world, more completely."

As it has since its inception in the mid-1990s, the organization leading the work continues to grow, change and morph to meet the challenge and shifting opportunities.

"For us, this continues to be an exciting journey," Weedman said. "We are learning as we go, and continually seeking ways to improve and tap into new opportunities. As we move forward, we are looking to expand our footprint and outreach globally, ensuring we're tapping the best minds regardless of their location. This means we need well-rounded and trained C+D experts in key regions around the world. We are doing this already, and they are working to expand their strategic networks. We're also working to build our internal networks—ensuring that our

C+D teams are intrinsically linked to the business—understanding and being able to react to their needs, strategies, and future directions.

"In addition, we're working to build—with deliberate care and planning—the networks that we've seen deliver the biggest value. This includes our connections with academia, where the biggest roadblock is often the time it takes to negotiate a partnership agreement. To address this, we are building collaboration agreements that include multiple universities, as we did with universities across Ohio and Michigan, and in Great Britain and Singapore. These master agreements enable faster connections and collaborations, which are a win for student innovators, for universities looking to attract top student talent, and for P&G as we tap into the energies and ideas of the schools with the possibility of opening new business opportunities. We also are looking to work more with government labs around the world, expand our work with venture capital firms, and look to build connections with small-to-medium enterprises, where much of today's innovation takes place.

"While each area offers a host of opportunities in itself, experience has shown us that each new door can lead to 15 to 20 others. And thus we are taking great care to work quickly—as the innovation clock ticks with accelerating speed —but deliberately, ensuring that we can develop relationships fully and deliver with excellence the opportunities that promise the biggest wins for the company, our partners and our global consumers."

Appendix A

Significant Developments in Intellectual Property Law in the Past 10 Years

Mark Radcliffe

This appendix summarizes the developments in intellectual property (IP) law in the United States in the first decade of the twenty-first century. This decade has been a dynamic period for IP law, and these changes reflect a number of important trends in the commercial markets that have driven these changes.

Recognition of Value of IP Rights

This decade reflects a dramatic increase in the understanding of businesses about the value of their IP and the need for corporate executives to manage the opportunities and the risks arising from IP. In a recent online survey of more than 630 U.S. and U.K. executives conducted by the consulting firm Accenture, more than 54 percent of the executives reported that their companies have a chief innovation officer or equivalent C-level position dedicated to innovation.

This change has been driven by six factors, which are described in the following sections.

Factor 1: Increase in IP Litigation and Damages

The dramatic increase in IP litigation and the increasing size of the judgments have made this area critical for business. According to a study by Navigant Consulting, the average size of the judgment in patent cases has increased each decade: In the 1980s, the average patent judgment was $6.2 million; in the 1990s, the average patent judgment was $13.2 million; in this decade (the study only covered 2000 to 2008), the average patent judgment was $17.8 million. In addition, the number of patents filed has increased from 295,926 in 2000 to 490,226 in 2010. However, these numbers do not reflect the enormous amount of the damages in some of these cases: $1.67 billion against Abbott Laboratories by Centocor for violation of patents relating to human antibodies (this judgment was recently overturned on appeal); $1.52 billion against Microsoft by Lucent in a patent case relating to digital music technology (the judgment was reversed and the parties settled for an undisclosed sum); and $1.3 billion against SAP by Oracle for violating its copyrights in Oracle's database software. The size of some of these judgments has attracted the attention of the business press and has been sufficient material to require the companies to report them under the Securities and Exchange Act of 1934. SAP's market value dropped 1 percent while Oracle's market value gained 2 percent on the day after the verdict.

In addition, IBM's patent licensing program was held up as a model for other companies in explaining IP. This program, which started in the early 1990s has consistently generated an average over $1 billion each year in license revenues for IBM during this decade. Eastman Kodak has been using the licensing of its over 1,000 digital imaging patents as an integral part of its transformation and has collected over $1.9 billion in royalties in the past three years (in 2010, Samsung paid Eastman Kodak a $550 million royalty payment after the International Trade Commission decision found that it violated Kodak's patent). The increasing complexity of products and the need for collaboration means that company's IP has become not only a stick with which they could beat their opponents, but also could serve as a bridge to encourage collaboration. The transformation of Microsoft from a "fortress" approach to IP to a more collaborative one is documented in Marshall Phelps' book *Burning the Ships*. He describes how Microsoft recognized the need to engage with other parties in order to remain successful in the world of increasingly rapid change. During Marshall Phelps's employment as Chief Intellectual Property Officer, Microsoft entered into over 500 technology agreements. Moreover, the average value of judgments in patent cases continues to increase dramatically in this decade.

Factor 2: Shift to Knowledge-Based Products and Collaborative Product Design

The value of IP has risen because of the fundamental shift in the nature of business to knowledge-based products such as software, computers, and digital commerce. For example, a WIPO report indicated that between 1982 and 2000, the physical assets of U.S. corporations declined from 62 percent of their value to 30 percent of their value. The U.S. economy, in particular, is increasingly focused on developing products such as software, semiconductors, and telecom equipment, where the IP rights are the most important method of defending these products. The importance of IP rights is also increased by the increasingly collaborative nature of product design in this decade: Most modern products are developed using components from multiple sources and thus, competitors may purchase these components on the open market and compete with the product developer unless that developer can defend its product using IP rights. For example, the bill of materials for the Apple iPhone listed in iSuppli.com makes clear that the software for the iPhone is the only component that is actually developed by Apple.

Factor 3: The Rise of the Internet

The increasing importance of the Internet to commerce is well documented. However, the Internet poses significant challenges to the IP system because of the way in which it operates and the ease of mass infringement. Virtually every action on the Internet, from caching a web page from a website by an Internet service provider to e-mailing an article is technically a copyright infringement unless licensed by the copyright owner (website terms and conditions play an important role in granting such permission). In addition, many parties participate in these potential infringements such as website owners, Internet service providers and payment services. Copyright law has long imposed liability on certain third parties who enable infringement but do not actually take the infringing action under the doctrines of contributory and vicarious infringement.

The Registrar of Copyright has summarized these issues before Congress as follows:

> For decades, courts have recognized that those who assist and facilitate copyright infringement are liable just as those who actually commit the acts of infringement. For example, in 1929 the Seventh Circuit Court of Appeals in *Dreamland Ballroom, Inc. vs. Shapiro, Bernstein & Co.*, held that a dance hall that hired an orchestra to provide music to its patrons was liable for the unauthorized public performance of musical works committed by that orchestra. That case is an example of "vicarious liability," which the landmark case of *Shapiro, Bernstein & Co. vs. H.L. Green Co.* explained this way:
>
> When the right and ability to supervise coalesce with an obvious and direct financial interest in the exploitation of copyrighted materials, the purposes of copyright law may be best effectuated by the imposition of liability upon the beneficiary of that exploitation.
>
> Thus, vicarious liability requires two elements: (1) the right and ability to supervise or control the infringing activity; and (2) a direct financial benefit from that activity. It is closely related to the doctrines of enterprise liability and respondeat superior in tort law.

There is another form of secondary liability in copyright law, "contributory infringement," which stretches back to 1911. As the Second Circuit Court of Appeals has explained, contributory infringement occurs where "[o]ne who, with knowledge of the infringing activity, induces, causes, or materially contributes to the infringing conduct of another." In general, the two elements of contributory infringement are (1) knowledge of the infringing activity; and (2) material contribution to the activity.

The Internet enables mass infringement on a scale unimaginable in the past and has substantially undercut the revenues of the music industry and may have a similar effect on the television and movie industry. Despite Congress' attempt to balance the conflict between copyright owners, users, and providers of Internet infrastructure (such as website owners and Internet service providers) in the Digital Millennium Copyright Act in 1998, these issues remain fiercely contested: from the multiple suits by the music industry against peer-to-peer networks such as Grokster and Limewire to the massive litigation between Viacom and YouTube over YouTube's liability for hosting videos whose copyrights are owned by Viacom.

The Internet also poses challenges for trademark law. Trademark permits the protection of the word, symbol, image, or sound to identify products or their quality and prevents other companies from adopting "confusingly similar" trademarks. The domain name system that is the basis for navigation on the Internet does not map to the trademark system. Trademark law permits multiple companies to use the same word for different products or services, such as Delta for (1) airlines (Delta Airlines), (2) dental services (Delta Dental), and (3) plumbing products (Delta Faucet). However, the domain system, designed by computer scientists, has only a single "Delta" in the dominant "dot-com" domain (i.e., a single www.delta.com). Trademark law, like all other IP law, is national in nature. In contrast, the Internet is borderless and "international." This difference adds another layer of conflict between trademark law and the domain system because some trademarks are owned by different, unrelated companies in different countries: for example, the trademark "Harrods" for a retail store services is owned by the Qatar Holdings in the United Kingdom, but an affiliate in Argentina was sold in the 1920s and the right to use Harrods for retail store services in Argentina is owned by Pérez Company (and a Swiss venture capital firm, CBC Interconfianz). Another common Internet practice, the sale of advertising based on "keywords" that are trademarks, raises issues of trademark infringement. If Google sells advertising to Panasonic Corporation when a user searches for "Sony" televisions, has either Google or Panasonic violated the trademark of Sony?

Factor 4: Reform of Patent Law

The current patent law in the United States has been the subject of significant criticism. This criticism arises from procedural issues such as moving from a "first-to-invent" system to the "first-to-file" system used throughout the rest of the world, to remedies such as how to calculate damages to the ability to obtain "injunctive relief." The last major revision to the patent law was passed by Congress in 1952. Despite wide agreement that the current patent law is antiquated and creates significant problems for U.S. business, Congress has not been able to enact patent reform. The Supreme Court has stepped into this void and become dramatically more active in deciding patent cases: From 1990 to 2000, the U.S. Supreme Court ("Supreme Court") agreed to review only six patent cases; from 2000 to 2010, the Supreme Court agreed to review 10 cases. And, the Supreme Court decisions ruled on fundamental issues about the scope of patent protection, the breadth of defenses to infringement and availability of injunctive relief as a remedy.

Factor 5: Rise of Software

Software has become ubiquitous, expanding from traditional functions such as accounting and word processing to control functions in products from automobiles to phones and medical devices. Yet software poses difficult challenges for traditional IP law: It is one of the few products that can be protected both by copyright and patent law. For copyright law, the functional nature of software poses significant challenges. Unlike traditional copyrightable works such as novels and films in which the author has wide freedom of choice, the choices in the development of software are limited by the need to work with other software (such as operating systems) and operate on certain hardware. These types of limitations do not apply to traditional products protected by copyright such as books, music, and film. Thus, copyright doctrines developed for such traditional products are difficult to apply to software. Yet these issues have become increasingly important as the value of software increases. In addition, the rise of free and open source software ("FOSS") makes previously obscure copyright issues of critical importance (such as the definition of "derivative work"), because most widely issued FOSS license, GNU General Public License version 2 ("GPLv2"), requires that all "derivative works" of the GPLv2 licensed software must be licensed under the terms of the GPLv2. Since the interaction between software programs can create a derivative work, companies need to carefully analyze how such proprietary software interacts with such GPLv2 licensed software. The importance of software was emphasized by the EU Commission's delay of the merger between Sun Microsystems, Inc., and Oracle Corporation based on the risk of making certain software products that Sun licensed under FOSS licenses—MySQL and Java—less freely available.

The availability (and scope) of patent protection for software continues to be very controversial. Although such protection has been available in the United States for some time, the European Patent Convention expressly excludes computer programs from patent protection although certain techniques can be used to obtain protection for computer programs as part of other products. During the decade, this issue has been hotly debated, with some countries permitting software patents and some rejecting them. The attempt to harmonize this approach was recently rejected by the European Parliament.

Factor 6: Rapidity of Change

This decade has seen increasing speed in product development and obsolescence; in such a world, a strong IP position can be critical to fending off potential competitors and extending the life of products. In addition, competition can arise from a variety of unexpected sources. The handset industry is an excellent example of this change. In 2007, Nokia's Symbian operating system was the dominant smartphone operating system with over a 60 percent share of the market. However, three years later, Symbian's share of the market had been reduced to 37 percent and the Symbian operating system had been abandoned by Nokia. Symbian had been displaced by Google's Android operating system (37 percent share of the market) and the Apple iPhone operating system (25 percent share of the market). Moreover, these two new operating systems were introduced by companies that were not handset manufacturers prior to their introduction. This disruption has resulted in 40 IP lawsuits over the Android operating system. These disputes led to a bidding war for the 6,000 Nortel patents between Google and a consortium of companies including Microsoft and Apple. The patents eventually sold for $4.5 billion.

Developments in Patent Law

The first decade of the twenty-first century has seen a significant increase in the number of patent lawsuits: A recent report by the law firm of Fulbright & Jaworski stated that in 2010, 29 percent of large companies (with over a billion dollars in market capitalization) were plaintiffs in patent litigation and 37 percent of these large companies were defendants. This period has also seen a dramatic increase in Supreme Court decisions relating to patent law, with the number of patent cases accepted for review by the Supreme Court doubling in this decade. These decisions are remarkable for their consistent limitation of the rights of patent holders. These decisions reflect the concern of the Supreme Court that the system had become tilted strongly towards patent holders, a new category of patent holders, nonpracticing entities (NPE) had arisen and Congress had been unable to reform the law.

The rise of NPE has had a very significant effect on the development of patent law. Many of these entities do not actually develop the patents that they enforce, but rather purchase them from failing businesses or, in some cases, from businesses that are pruning their patent portfolio. One NPE, Acacia Research, Inc., is public: it has filed 337 patent related lawsuits over the past eighteen years and has increased its revenues from $34.8 million in 2006 to $153 million in 2010. More recently, Nathan Myrvold, the former CTO of Microsoft Corporation, has set up a company to purchase patents, Intellectual Ventures (IV). IV is reported to have raised over $5 billion and purchased over 30,000 patents (IV is private so this information cannot be verified). Although IV for many years claimed that they would not sue companies for infringement that policy changed in 2011 when IV filed its first lawsuits.

The rise of patent trolls and their influence is reflected in Justice Kennedy's concurring opinion in *eBay vs. MercExhange* case, another case brought by a patent troll:

> In cases now arising trial courts should bear in mind that in many instances the nature of the patent being enforced and the economic function of the patent holder present considerations quite unlike earlier cases. An industry has developed in which firms use patents not as a basis for producing and selling goods but, instead, primarily for obtaining licensing fees. See FTC, To Promote Innovation: The Proper Balance of Competition and Patent Law and Policy, ch. 3, pp. 38–39 (Oct. 2003), available at www.ftc.gov/os/2003/10/innovationrpt.pdf (as visited May 11, 2006, and available in Clerk of Court's case file). For these firms, an injunction, and the potentially serious sanctions arising from its violation, can be employed as a bargaining tool to charge exorbitant fees to companies that seek to buy licenses to practice the patent. See ibid. When the patented invention is but a small component of the product the companies seek to produce the threat of an injunction is employed simply for undue leverage in negotiations, legal damages may well be sufficient to compensate for the infringement 397*397 and an injunction may not serve the public interest. In addition injunctive relief may have different consequences for the burgeoning number of patents over business methods, which were not of much economic and legal significance in earlier times. The potential vagueness and suspect validity of some of these patents may affect the calculus under the four-factor test.

The coercive power of patent trolls under the patent law at the beginning of the decade was very publicly demonstrated in the dispute between NTP Inc. ("NTP") and Research in Motion, Ltd. ("RIM"). NTP had developed certain patents in wireless technology, but its business model was not to manufacture products but rather to collect royalties from handset manufacturers. RIM developed and manufactures the BlackBerry handset. After negotiations failed, NTP filed a lawsuit against RIM in 2001. A jury found NTP's patents to be valid and that RIM had willfully infringed the patents. The jury rewarded NTP a $33 million compensatory damages that the judge increased to $52 million. The court also granted a permanent injunction that prohibited RIM from making, using, or selling BlackBerry devices with the NTP functionality. During the appeal, the Department of Justice (and later the Department of Defense) filed briefs with the court stating that shutting down the BlackBerry service would be severely detrimental to the Federal government and would adversely affect national security. After the failure of the appeal to the Court of Appeals of the Federal Circuit ("CAFC") and a rejection of an appeal to the Supreme Court and under the threat of the injunction, RIM settled the dispute for $612 million. This amount was more than 20 times the amount of compensatory damages awarded by the jury.

Five decisions of the Supreme Court from the last decade illustrate this more activist approach to patent law. It is noteworthy that these cases are remarkably free of dissent (several of them were unanimous) and four out of five of these cases clearly ruled against the patent holder, reducing the scope of the patentable inventions, limiting remedies and expanding the scope of defenses, as well as the strength of the remedies available to the patent holder. *Bilski vs. Kappos*, the fifth (and most recent) case was also decided against the patent holder, but is less broad in its application.

KSR International Company vs. Teleflex, Inc.: Reducing the Scope of Patent Applications

The Supreme Court in the *KSR International Company ("KSR") vs. Teleflex Inc.* ("Teleflex") decision unanimously found that the CAFC was interpreting the "obviousness" requirement under the Patent Act for protection too narrowly. All utility patents must meet three tests: usefulness, nonobviousness, and novelty. Obviousness has been a difficult concept for the courts to determine. However, it is critical to the scope of patents because Section 103 of the Patent Act forbids the issuance of a patent "when differences between the subject matter sought to be patented and the prior art are such that the subject matter as a whole would have been obvious at the time the invention was made to a person having ordinary skill in the art to which said such subject matter pertains."

The patent in the Teleflex case covered a mechanism for combining "an electronic sensor with an adjustable automobile pedal, so the pedal's position could be transferred to the computer that controls the throttle in the vehicle's engine." Teleflex sued KSR, accusing KSR of adding an electronic sensor to one of KSR's previously designed pedals and thus, infringing Teleflex's patents.

The CAFC had developed a test to provide more consistency in determining whether a combination invention is "nonobvious":

> . . . "teaching, suggestion, or motivation" test (TSM test), under which a patent claim is only proved obvious if "some motivation or suggestion to combine the prior art teachings" can be found in the prior art, the nature of the problem, or the knowledge of a person having ordinary skill in the art.

The Supreme Court rejected this test.

> We begin by rejecting the rigid approach of the Court of Appeals. Throughout this Court's engagement with the question of obviousness, our cases have set forth an expansive and flexible approach inconsistent with the way the Court of Appeals applied its TSM test here.

Although the decision left the scope of obviousness ambiguous, it signaled to the lower courts that they should be more aggressive in applying the obviousness doctrine to invalidate patents. Many commentators stated that the decision made it much easier to invalidate patents based on obviousness. In fact, Michael Barclay of Wilson Sonsini Goodrich & Rosati, an experienced patent litigator, described the decision as "the most important patent case of the last 20 years." He noted that every litigated patent case includes an assertion of obviousness and that the decision should help stem the flow of patents of questionable value based on it being issued by the patent and trademark office. He described obviousness as the most important legal gateway to patenting and the decision could potentially affect patents with trillions of dollars in value.

e-Bay vs. Merc Exchange: Limiting Remedies

e-Bay vs. MercExchange LLC was one of the Supreme Court's first decisions to deal with the problems posed by patent trolls, and it fundamentally altered one of the fundamental assumptions in the patent troll business model. The business model of patent trolls is very dependent on the threat of injunctive relief (a court order prohibiting use of the invention) to persuade defendants to pay large settlements: for example, the "settlement" damages in the BlackBerry case were 20 times the "actual" damages.

MercExchange, LLC ("MercExchange"), a patent troll, tried to license its business method patent to eBay and its subsidiary, Half.com, which covered "an electronic market designed to facilitate the sale of goods between private individuals by establishing a central authority to promote trust among participants." After eBay refused to negotiate, MercExchange sued eBay for infringement and the jury found that MercExchange patents were valid and they had been willfully infringed. Although the CAFC had ruled that the "general rule" is to grant injunctive relief when infringement is found, the District Court refused to grant an injunction prohibiting eBay from using the inventions in MercExchange's patents. The District Court based its decision on MercExchange's willingness to license its patent and its lack of its commercial activity. On that basis, the District Court found that MercExchange would not suffer "irreparable harm" if the injunction was not granted. The CAFC referred to its prior decisions and reversed the District Court. The CAFC granted an injunction against eBay to MercExchange. The CAFC indicated that injunctions should be denied only in the "unusual" case, under "exceptional circumstances" and "in rare instances . . . to protect the public interest."

The Supreme Court heard the case in early 2006 and unanimously reversed the CAFC decision (and rejected reasoning of the District Court as too broad). The Supreme Court made clear that CAFC's "general rule" of granting injunctions was incorrect. Instead, the Supreme Court gave

District Courts significant discretion in granting or denying injunctive relief. The Supreme Court required that the grant of a permanent injunction on the patent holder was subject to the traditional requirements of injunctive relief and the patent holder must prove that: "(1) it has suffered an irreparable injury; (2) the legal remedy is inadequate; (3) the balance of hardships between the parties favors the injunction; (4) the public interest would not be disturbed by the injunction." These factors are similar to those proposed by Congress in its draft Patent Reform Act, which was not adopted during that session of Congress. Upon remand, the District Court again denied granting injunctive relief.

The results of this decision can be illustrated in two cases involving Microsoft Corporation that were decided soon after the MercExchange decision. Both cases: *z4 Technologies Inc. ("z4") vs. Microsoft Corporation*, and *Microsoft Corp. vs. i4i Limited Partnership ("i4i")* were decided in the Eastern District of Texas, a district that is generally very favorable to patent holders. In the z4 case, the district court found infringement and awarded damages, but did not grant a preliminary injunction. On the other hand, the district court awarded both damages and injunctive relief to i4i. The major difference between the cases was the status of the patent owner: z4 owned patents developed by its founder, but did not distribute a product based on the patent. In contrast, i4i was a company using its patent in its own products and did not license its patent. These differences are so striking that they merit a more detailed review.

z4 owned two patents on the prevention of software piracy. After negotiations with Microsoft failed, z4 sued Microsoft and several other companies. The jury found that Microsoft willfully infringed the patents and awarded z4 $115 million in damages that the court increased by an additional $25 million. However z4 was not successful in obtaining a permanent injunction that would have required Microsoft to disable the infringing functions in its programs. The court found that to do so Microsoft would have to rerelease its current versions of Office, with 450 separate variations in 37 different languages, and Windows, with 600 separate variations in over 40 languages. Microsoft contends that both products would have to be reengineered, tested, repackaged, and then placed into the appropriate distribution channels. According to Microsoft, such an undertaking would require excessive resources and be exceedingly expensive. The district court stated:

There is no logical reason that a potential consumer or licensee of z4's technology would have been dissuaded from purchasing or licensing z4's product activation technology for use in its own software due to Microsoft's infringement. Similarly, Microsoft's continued infringement does not inhibit z4's ability to market, sell, or license its patented technology to other entities in the market. Microsoft does not produce product activation software that it then individually sells, distributes, or licenses to other software manufacturers or consumers. If it did, then z4 might suffer irreparable harm in that Microsoft would be excluding z4 from selling or licensing its technology to those software manufacturers or consumers. However, Microsoft only uses the infringing technology as a small component of its own software, and it is not likely that any consumer of Microsoft's Windows or Office software purchases these products for their product activation functionality.

The district court went on to note:

In his concurrence, Justice Kennedy instructed courts to be cognizant of the nature of the patent being enforced and the economic function of the patent holder when applying the equitable factors. Id. at 1842 (Kennedy, J., concurring). Justice Kennedy specifically mentioned the situation where a "patented invention is but a small component of the product the companies seek to produce" and states that in such a situation, "legal damages may well be sufficient to compensate for the infringement and an injunction may not serve the public interest." Id. (Kennedy, J., concurring). Here, product activation is a very small component of the Microsoft Windows and Office software products that the jury found to infringe z4's patents. The infringing product activation component of the software is in no way related to the core functionality for which the software is purchased by consumers. Accordingly, Justice Kennedy's comments support the conclusion that monetary damages would be sufficient to compensate z4 for any future infringement by Microsoft.

In contrast, i4i brought suit against Microsoft Corporation ("Microsoft"), alleging that the custom XML editor in certain versions of Microsoft Word ("Word"), infringed i4i's patent. After a seven-day trial, the jury found Microsoft liable for willful infringement. The jury rejected Microsoft's argument that the patent was invalid and awarded $200 million in damages to i4i. Although statutorily authorized to triple the jury's damages award because of Microsoft's willful infringement, the district court awarded only $40 million in additional damages. It also granted i4i's motion for a permanent injunction. This injunction was stayed pending the outcome of an appeal to the CAFC. The CAFC affirmed the grant of the injunction based on the district court's interpretation of the MercExchange factor:

> The district court found that before and after Microsoft began infringing, i4i produced and sold software that practiced the patented method. The district court found no evidence that i4i had previously licensed the patent, instead finding evidence that i4i sought to retain exclusive use of its invention.

In this case, a small company was practicing its patent, only to suffer a loss of market share, brand recognition, and customer goodwill as the result of the defendant's infringing acts. Such losses may frequently defy attempts at valuation, particularly when the infringing acts significantly change the relevant market, as occurred here. The district court found that Microsoft captured 80 percent of the custom XML market with its infringing Word products, forcing i4i to change its business strategy:

> The district court found that i4i's business is comprised "almost exclusively" of products based on the '449 patent. In contrast, Microsoft's infringing custom XML editor was found to be "merely one of thousands of features" within Word, used by only a small fraction of Microsoft's customers. The district court further found that Microsoft's infringement of the '449 patent allowed Microsoft to "corner[] the XML market."

The Supreme Court affirmed the decision in favor of i4i. The MercExchange decision radically altered the remedies available to patent holders. However, this effect is particularly important for NPEs because they can no longer rely on leverage from potential injunctions to obtain large license fees.

Quanta Computer, Inc., vs. LG Electronics, Inc.: Expanding Defenses

The *Quanta Computer, Inc., ("Quanta") vs. LG Electronics, Inc. ("LG")* case expanded the defense patent exhaustion. The patent exhaustion doctrine terminates the rights of a patent owner over infringing products after the product is sold in an unconditional and authorized sale. The basis for the patent exhaustion doctrine is to limit the patent owner from obtaining double royalties (i.e., royalties from both the direct purchaser and the downstream purchaser of the product). This defense has become more important.

The Quanta case arises from the trend for products to be based on components from numerous third parties: it involves a suit against a manufacturer (Quanta) for use of components for use with Intel microprocessors. LG licensed three method patents to Intel for the use and management of data in computers. The license agreement expressly stated that no license would be granted to third parties to make combinations of the Intel microprocessors and other components from parties other than LG or Intel. The license stated that no license:

> is granted by either party hereto . . . to any third party for the combination by a third party of Licensed Products of either party with items, components, or the like acquired . . . from sources other than a party hereto, or for the use, import, offer for sale or sale of such combination.

In addition, LG and Intel had entered into a separate agreement in which Intel agreed to provide written notice to its customers of the limited scope of Intel's licensing right to LG's patents. In an unusual provision, the license agreement expressly stated that it did not alter the effect of the patent exhaustion doctrine.

Quanta purchased microprocessor and chipsets from Intel using LG's patented method and received the written notice. The notice explained that Quanta was not authorized to use the Intel products with non-Intel components or to sell such combinations. Quanta, nonetheless, combined these Intel microprocessors and chipsets with non-Intel components to build its computer systems for sale. LG sued Quanta for patent infringement. The district court granted summary judgment in favor of Quanta, holding that for purposes of patent exhaustion, the sale by Intel was approved by LG and was without restriction. However, upon review, the district court reversed itself to find that patent exhaustion did not apply to method patents and granted summary judgment to LG rather than Quanta. The CAFC upheld this decision in 2006.

In 2008 the Supreme Court granted review and unanimously reversed the CAFC decision. The Supreme Court stated:

> In this case, we decide whether patent exhaustion applies to the sale of components of a patented system that must be combined with additional components in order to practice the patented methods. The Court of Appeals for the Federal Circuit held that the doctrine does not apply to method patents at all and, in the alternative that it does not apply here because the sales were not authorized by the license agreement. We disagree on both scores. Because the exhaustion doctrine applies to method patents, and because the license authorizes the sale of components that substantially embody the patents in suit, the sale exhausted the patents.

Upon remand to the district court, Quanta filed for summary judgment of noninfringement and won. This case demonstrates the Supreme Court's desire to limit the rights of patent holders: The expansion of the scope of a traditional defense is one approach.

Medimmune, Inc., vs. Genentech, Inc.: Encouraging Challenges to Patent Validity

The Supreme Court in the *Medimmune Inc. vs. Genentech Inc.* case reversed decades of precedent to permit licensees to challenge the validity of the licensed patents while keeping the license. The case is very important because the companies who have the greatest economic incentive to challenge the validity of a patent are companies who are paying royalties under a patent license. Although this rule would seem to be common sense, the U.S. Constitution requires that courts only decide "cases and controversies" and not "hypothetical cases." This doctrine is embodied in a general rule under common law "that a party to a contract cannot at one and the same time challenge its validity and continue to reap its benefits." Thus, prior to the *Medimmune* decision, courts required that, in order to challenge the validity of a licensed patent, a licensee "(i) actually ceases payment of royalties, and (ii) provides notice to the licensor that the reason for ceasing payment of royalties is because it has deemed the relevant claims to be invalid." Such actions will generally result in the termination of the license by the licensor, thus giving the licensee a very difficult choice. If the licensee is wrong about the validity of the patent, the termination of the license means that the licensee may be subject to damages and injunctive relief. The practical result was that very few licensees would challenge the validity of patents that they had licensed.

The *Medimmune* case involved a license between Genentech and Medimmune (Genentech was operating on behalf of the City of Hope Medical Center) in which certain "chimeric antibodies" were licensed to Medimmune. In 2001, a patent application under the license became a patent and Genentech demanded royalties based on the newly issued patent. Medimmune responded that the patent was invalid and nonenforceable and then filed a declaratory relief action in the courts that such royalties were not due.

Overturning many decades of precedent, the Supreme Court found that this dispute over the invalidity of the patent was sufficient to be a "case or controversy" under the U.S. Constitution and that Medimmune did not have to cease to pay royalties and announce its reason to challenge the validity of the patent. Consequently the *Medimmune* case substantially reduces the value of a patent from a licensing perspective because the patent can always be challenged by the licensee without terminating the license agreement.

Bilski vs. Kappos: Limiting the Scope of Patentable Inventions

The most recent case, *Bilski vs. Kappos*, was decided in 2010. The case dealt with the patentability of a business process that "claims a procedure for instructing buyers and sellers how to protect against the risk of price fluctuations in a discrete section of the economy." The CAFC had initially expanded the scope of processes that were patentable in the 1990s, but starting in the early part of this decade reversed course and adopted the "machine or transformation" test that limited the scope of processes that were found patentable.

The Supreme Court chose not to rule that "business processes" were not patentable (many "friends" of the court requested such a ruling), because "process" is in the Patent Act. Thus, the Supreme Court stated that "business processes" were patentable if they met their relevant standards of the patent law. The Supreme Court agreed that the "machine or transformation" test was the primary (but not the only) test for determining the patentability of processes.

Although the majority decision suggested a strong desire to limit the types of processes that would be patentable, the majority did not change the standard. In fact, one commentator described the decision as "business as usual." However, the concurring opinion showed that some of the members of the Supreme Court wished to impose significant additional limits on patentability of business processes:

> But the Court is quite wrong, in my view, to suggest that any series of steps that is not itself an abstract idea or law of nature may constitute a "process" within the meaning of § 101. The language in the Court's opinion to this effect can only cause mischief. The wiser course would have been to hold that petitioners' method is not a "process" because it describes only a general method of engaging in business transactions—and business methods are not patentable. More precisely, although a process is not patent-ineligible simply because it is useful for conducting business, a claim that merely describes a method of doing business does not qualify as a "process" under § 101.

Developments in Copyright Law

Copyright law played a much broader role in society during the past decade because of its application to the Internet and software that became ubiquitous. Yet the development of copyright law was quite different from patent law: unlike patent law, the scope of copyright law generally expanded. The Internet has posed a particular challenge for copyright law because the manner in which the Internet operates is frequently based on copyright infringement: The performance of music on websites violates the public performance right under copyright law of the musical composition and the "caching" of web pages by Internet service providers to make them available to third parties violates the rights of copyright holders of the text, video and images on such web pages. And the Internet provides a platform for massive copyright infringement, such as the music distribution enabled by Napster and Grokster. The infringement enabled by these peer-to-peer networks has dramatically undercut the revenues of the music industry.

Copyright law imposes liability on the persons who actually violate one or more of the five rights under copyright law: reproduction, distribution, modification, public performance, and public display. These infringements may be limited through defenses such as fair use. The person who violates these rights is a "direct" infringer. Thus, the person who makes a copy of a webpage is a "direct infringer." However, copyright law also imposes liability on third parties who enable the "direct infringer" in certain ways. The scope of liability for such "indirect liability" had been an obscure area of copyright law prior to the advent of the Internet. The most frequent cases involved restaurants and bars who played music for which the performers did not have a public performance license. One exception to this rule was the challenge by movie studios against Sony for indirect infringement because of the copying of movies by individuals enabled by Sony's videocassette recorders (the movie studios lost). However, these cases were rare.

The ability of the Internet to permit massive copying radically altered the view of courts about the liability for the third parties who enabled such copying. The first such case was against an Internet service provider in San Jose, California, for hosting a message board that included infringing documents. The court was clearly concerned in applying traditional copyright law doctrines to this situation because of the widespread implications. However, the case settled. At that time, the courts had two doctrines to apply to indirect infringements: contributory infringement and vicarious infringement. Contributory infringement imposes liability upon a party when the party has "knowledge" of the direct infringement and materially contributes to the infringement. However, this doctrine does not apply if the product has "substantially noninfringing uses." Sony won the challenge to its videocassette recorders because the Supreme Court found that the "time shifting" of television programs by users was a substantial non-infringing use. Vicarious infringement imposes liability on a third party based on the ability of the party to exercise control over the direct infringement and receipt of a direct financial benefit from such infringement.

The first major dispute in this area involved a direct infringer: MP3.com copied 45,000 albums into its servers to provide a "virtual jukebox" to its customers (who needed to "own" a copy of the album to have it streamed to them). MP3.com was sued by all of the major record labels and paid over $150 million in settlements and damages. However, MP3.com was eclipsed by Napster: Napster hosted a form of peer-to-peer networks that enabled individuals to download music or share music for free with other users of the service. The court found Napster liable as a contributory infringer because of the "centralized" listing of songs available for sharing that Napster controlled and Napster filed for bankruptcy.

However, the newer peer-to-peer networks had no central listing and the traditional theories of indirect infringement did not easily apply to those situations. The Supreme Court was considering these issues when it decided the *MGM Studios, Inc., vs. Grokster* case. The Supreme Court expanded copyright law by creating a new theory of indirect liability, inducement (borrowing from a similar doctrine in patent law). In this case, the Supreme Court found that Grokster had induced infringement because of the evidence of Grokster's intention to encourage infringement in order to make money on advertisements. The decision eventually caused Grokster to shut down. This theory significantly expanded the scope of copyright in the context of the Internet. In fact, one company, Perfect 10, has tried to extend this indirect liability to include Internet service providers and even credit-card companies who permit payment for photographs that Perfect 10 claims are infringing. These claims have been rejected by the courts.

Congress addressed this tension between the rights of copyright owners and the third parties, such as Internet service providers, who help run the Internet through the Digital Millennium Copyright Act ("DMCA") in 1998. The DMCA provided exemptions from monetary liability for "service providers" (primarily Internet service providers and websites) if they undertook certain steps and fit into one of four categories. Unfortunately, major issues under the DMCA remain uncertain and major litigation continues about its scope.

The most significant case was brought by Viacom against YouTube, the video hosting site. In one day, Viacom identified over 100,000 infringing videos (YouTube had removed them by the next day). Nonetheless, Viacom sued YouTube claiming that YouTube is:

> . . . not protected by the statutory "safe harbor" provision, but is "liable for the intentional infringement of thousands of Viacom's copyrighted works, . . . for the vicarious infringement of those works, and for the direct infringement of those works . . . because: (1) Defendants had 'actual knowledge' and were 'aware of facts and circumstances from which infringing activity [was] apparent,' but failed to 'act[] expeditiously' to stop it; (2) Defendants 'receive[d] a financial benefit directly attributable to the infringing activity' and 'had the right and ability to control such activity;' and (3) Defendants' infringement does not result solely from providing 'storage at the direction of a user' or any other Internet function specified in section 512."

In 2010, the district court found that YouTube had complied with the requirements of the DMCA and was immune to monetary damages, but the case is on appeal. In fact, Google recognized these potential issues and set aside $200 million of the $1.3 billion price that it paid for YouTube for potential legal liability.

The Internet also poses challenges to the scope of traditional copyright law doctrines such as "fair use." The most dramatic is Google's attempt to develop a "universal library," known as the Google Library Project that started in 2004. Google agreed with university libraries to digitize their collections (but without permission from the authors). Although Google copied all of the books, they agreed to make only "limited amounts" available to the public and relied on a "fair use" defense. The Copyright Office describes "fair use" as follows:

> Section 107 contains a list of the various purposes for which the reproduction of a particular work may be considered fair, such

as criticism, comment, news reporting, teaching, scholarship, and research. Section 107 also sets out four factors to be considered in determining whether or not a particular use is fair: (1) the purpose and character of the use, including whether such use is of commercial nature or is for nonprofit educational purposes; (2) the nature of the copyrighted work; (3) the amount and substantiality of the portion used in relation to the copyrighted work as a whole; and (4) the effect of the use upon the potential market for, or value of, the copyrighted work.

After extensive negotiations, a group of authors and publishers sued Google as a class to prevent Google's digitizing the books and making them available. In 2009, the parties entered into a complicated settlement in which U.S. authors received compensation through a system of registration if first published in the United States, UK, Canada, or Australia. The settlement also provided for separate compensation for other works in books such as photographs and illustrations. The settlement seemed ready to radically transform copyright law. However, in March 2011 a court rejected the settlement and the future of the settlement (and Google's Library Project) is unclear.

Software was the other major source of challenges for copyright law. Copyright law was initially developed for creative works such as music, film, and books. However, software is fundamentally different from such works because it is functional: The options in developing software are constrained by a number of factors such as the hardware on which it is written, the operating system for which it is written and other technical factors. Traditional copyright law doctrines are not well-suited to deal with this type of functional product.

The enormous value of software in the economy means that the scope of protection for software is important. The need for clarity on this issue has become more urgent because of the increasing use of free and open-source software (FOSS). FOSS is licensed under a variety of fixed licenses. FOSS is ubiquitous and is widely used by both businesses and consumers. For example, the Apache web servers are used on 60 percent of web servers even though it is competing with products from IBM and Microsoft. The Linux operating system is used in products ranging from television sets to automobiles to cell phones. In 2010, Accenture reported that open source software had "crossed the chasm" and become part of the IT infrastructure of most companies.

The most commonly used FOSS license is the GNU General Public License version 2 (GPLv2) which is "copyleft." GPLv2 requires that any software "based on" on the GPLv2 licensed software must also be distributed under GPLv2. GPLv2 requires that, upon distribution, the licensor must make the source code of its software available for free to its licensees and permit the licensee to modify and distribute the software at no charge. Many proprietary companies are very concerned about integrating their valuable proprietary software with software licensed under GPLv2 because of the risk that their proprietary code would be subject to the GPLv2. Thus, if the proprietary software is subject to these obligations, such software will lose a significant amount of its value. This issue has risen most recently in the claim that the Android operating system violates the GPLv2 because it integrates the Linux kernel with other components in the Android operating system in a way that requires all of the Android operating system to be distributed under the GPLv2.

The significant economic value of software means that these questions will continue to be critical to the development of copyright law.

Developments in Trademark Law

Trademark law was most affected by the challenges arising due to the rise of the Internet. Like copyright and patent, trademark law is a national law, yet the Internet is borderless so that all use of trademarks is fundamentally international. Trademark law faces a particular challenge because of the mismatch between trademark law and the Internet's address system of "domain names." This mismatch is fundamental and is not likely to be resolved easily.

Disputes over these conflicts continued through the first decade of the twenty-first century. In 1999, the U. S. Congress enacted a law to prohibit "domain name" pirates, the Anticybersquatting Consumer Protection Act (ACPA). The ACPA provides that "a party can be held liable if it registers, traffics in, or uses a 'domain name' that is identical or confusingly similar to a distinctive mark . . . with a bad faith intent to profit from the mark." However, the difficulty of resolving these issues by legislation was demonstrated by a recent case between GoForIt Entertainment, LLC, and DigiMedia.com, LP, CyberFusion.com LP, Hapidays, Inc., DigiMedia.com Management, Inc., and Scott Day. The plaintiff, GoForIt Entertainment LLC (GFI), asserted that the defendant's use of "GoForIt" within their domain names violated GFI's trademark rights as well as violating ACPA. The defendants used "GoForIt" as part of third level domain www.goforit.org.com (first-level domains are www.goforit .com owned by GFI). The value of these domain names is increased by the "Auto complete" function in many browsers that permits the entry of "http://www" in the beginning and ".org" to the end, after which the browser will go to the defendant's domain name. The court found the defendants not liable despite numerous theories: violation of Lanham Act for cyberpiracy, the violation of the ACPA, service mark infringement, unfair competition, common-law trademark infringement, and common-law unfair competition in Texas. The court found that the use of the third level domains by the defendants was outside the ACPA because the "third level domain" was not "registered" with or assigned by a "domain name registrar" as required under the ACPA.

The second challenge for trademark law is the use of trademarks by search engines such as Google to sell "advertising" that may be purchased by a trademark owner's competitors. In traditional trademark law, the use of a trademark to advertise a good or service incurs liability, but the "accurate" use of a trademark by a retailer to sell the trademarked product is not "use" and not prohibited by trademark law. The use of trademarks by search engines to generate advertising does not easily fit in a particular category. The Google AdWords program is best known and has been challenged in many cases. At one time Google was defending thirteen separate cases against its "AdWords" program. Google had been able to win or settle these claims. However, in 2010 and early 2011, Google had two significant victories in the U.S. In 2010, the court gave a very expansive victory in a case involving Rosetta Stone, the provider of software programs for language learning. Upon summary judgment, the court rejected all of the theories proposed by Rosetta Stone to impose liability on Google. A victory by summary judgment is significant because the standard for summary judgment imposes a heavy burden on the party moving for it. The court stated that

Google's intent to "profit" was insufficient to incur liability and dismissed Rosetta Stone's survey claiming "confusion" among customers about whether the advertising was authorized by Rosetta Stone (the court noted that five examples of confusion out of 100,000,000 impressions was de minimus). This case is on appeal and major companies such as Ford Motor Company, Monster Cable, and 1-800 Contacts are taking Rosetta Stone's side.

In 2011, Google had another success in a case brought by GEICO. The court found that the use of the GEICO by Google to sell advertising to third parties under the AdWords program was not trademark infringement. However the courts also noted that the use of the GEICO trademark in the "sponsored links" section of the search might be trademark infringement and remanded that to the district court for further decision. This case indicates the importance of seemingly minor factual issues.

However, a recent decision in California muddies these issues for Google. The court did not find Google liable, but did find the purchase of the "keyword" that was a registered trademark was trademark infringement. Ironically, the case involved the use of the name of a law firm, Binder & Binder, by their competitors. The court awarded damages to Binder & Binder of $292,000. It's not clear if this decision will be followed in other jurisdictions.

Despite Google's success in the United States, its record overseas has more mixed results. By 2010, one commentator noted:[1]

> So far, there have been more than 70 decisions on Adwords in EU member states, more than 30 in France alone. The rulings differ in finding and reasoning. The use of trademark protected terms as keywords may be legal in some member states (e.g., in Great Britain), may be illegal in other member states (e.g., in France and Italy). German courts are split on this question.

These decisions have become less important because of a decision by the European Court of Justice in the spring of 2010 which stated that the advertiser purchasing a keyword which is protected by trademark potentially liable for trade mark infringement by use of the adwords, but Google is not liable for the act of selling/hosting the Adword program unless it has knowledge of infringing use to be made by the advertiser use of trademarks for keyword:[2]

> We believe that user interest is best served by maximizing the choice of keywords, ensuring relevant and informative advertising for a wide variety of different contexts. For instance, if a user is searching for information about a particular car, he or she will want more than just that car's website. They might be looking for different dealers that sell that car, secondhand cars, reviews about the car or looking for information about other cars in the same category.

These challenges to trademark law are likely to continue for the next decade.

Appendix B

The Rise of
Patent Aggregators

Kent Richardson and Erik Oliver

I t is important to have a common terminology for this discussion. The following terms are provided for your reference.

Terminology

Nonpracticing entity (NPE)—an entity—for example, a company, partnership, non-profit, government agency, or limited liability corporation (LLC)—that holds patents for which the entity does not currently produce a product, or have plans to do so, embodying the patented inventions. There are many different kinds of NPEs with many different business models. Examples include universities, LLCs set up to litigate a select group of patents, and corporations whose stated goal is to help inventors monetize their patents through assertion (e.g., Acacia Research Corporation [NASDAQ: ACTG]).

Patent aggregator—an entity whose primary business function is to buy patents outright or purchase licenses to patents. Examples include Intellectual Ventures (IV), Rational Patent Exchange (RPX), and Acacia.

Patent assertion entity (PAE)—a new term recently coined by the Federal Trade Commission (FTC) in their March 2011 report on the evolving IP marketplace,[1] a PAE "refer(s) to firms whose business model primarily focuses on purchasing and asserting patents." One way to contrast PAEs with NPEs is that NPEs may have technology development and deployment as a significant component of their business models even though NPEs may not ultimately practice the patented technology. Examples include Acacia and Intellectual Ventures.

Patent troll—a derogatory term originally used to describe NPEs and PAEs.[2] The problem with the term *patent troll* is that it is not particularly descriptive. It raises emotional responses but fails to differentiate among the different business models. Today, the term *patent troll* has become part of the vernacular of the public press, but is not used by patent licensing insiders—the discourse is moving beyond name-calling and into analysis of business models.

It's important to understand that these definitions are not necessarily mutually exclusive. For example, Intellectual Ventures can be described as a PAE, an NPE and a patent aggregator. Throughout this chapter, the terms NPE, patent aggregator, and PAE are used as defined here.

Background

Taken collectively, patent aggregators, NPEs, and PAEs in the information technology, computer, electrical, and semiconductor space have led to significant concerns of impeded technology progress and unfair taxing of technology development. The concerns have produced lobbying for patent reform, caused the Federal Trade Commission to conduct extensive hearings and issue a report, created an industry of patent litigation studies (e.g., PWC Patent Litigation Study), and led academics, such as Mark Lemley, to produce studies and policy papers on the topic.

Patent Aggregators in History

Some historical perspective on patent aggregation is useful when examining the patent aggregation marketplace today. In many respects, everything old is new again. Patent aggregation and assertion have been going on since the start of the U.S. Patent Office. What has changed recently is the size and scale of the activities—it is an interesting time (sometimes it is "interesting" in the sense of the purported Chinese curse).

Major technological development has always been marked with major patent battles. The cotton gin, the steam engine, power generation and distribution, the telephone, and the television all drove significant technological development, and all experienced significant patent assertion activity.[3] Each of these major technological developments experienced patent assertions, patent litigations, patent aggregations, and calls for reform and fairness in the patent system.

More recently, the semiconductor industry has experienced the transition from older patent assertion and licensing models to the current models. When deconstructed, the basic business models compared to the historic patent aggregation models do not differ; the size and scale is what has changed.

The following history of patent licensing practices in the semiconductor industry is taken from in-person stories told to us by people who were there at the time.

In the early days of the semiconductor business (late 1960s to early 1980s), semiconductor companies cross-licensed each other without much focus on the underlying patents.[4] The cross licenses tended to be simple—one-page licenses covering thousands of patents. This did create a barrier for those companies coming later to the business, but patents were not foremost in the minds of the semiconductor executives.[5]

The late 1980s and early 1990s brought changes to the semiconductor business. Japanese companies began aggressively competing with U.S. semiconductor companies. Intel exited the memory market because of fierce competition. Combined with changes in patent law (in particular, the creation of the dedicated patent appeals court), patent licensing practices changed. Texas Instruments and others began using their patents to effectively charge a fee to latecomers to the semiconductor business.

These patent assertion activities are often referred to as the "patent stack height" or "inches of patents" negotiations. The story, as told by many, is that both sides would meet at the negotiation table, stack their printed-out patents and compare the heights. The company with the shorter stack would pay the company with the taller stack. It was even suggested that the payments were based upon a fixed dollar amount per inch in difference. For those in the patent licensing business, this seems surprisingly simplistic and incredible. And in many respects this story is inaccurate.

In reality, the patent assertion happened much as it does today. One side presented its best patents, the other side then tried to knock those patents out by showing that the patents were invalid, not infringed, or unenforceable. Over multiple meetings, each side's list of asserted patents grew or shrank, depending on the efficacy of their teams and the quality of the patent assertions. At the end of the discussions, one side would have substantially more patents left on the table than the other side. The winner would then receive a patent license payment.[6]

Primarily in the semiconductor and mobile phone markets, the patent assertion and defense practices matured throughout the 1990s. Leading patent licensors included Texas Instruments, Qualcomm, and IBM. These practices became the model for patent assertions in other high technology areas. The model provided significant financial returns for those companies that implemented it and the internal patent licensing teams became experts. In the 2000s, these teams began to leave their corporations to start patent aggregation and licensing businesses. For example, Intellectual Ventures was created by some of the key IP team members from IBM and Intel.

Today, semiconductor, software, cloud computing, web, and software as a service (SaaS) businesses all face patent assertions not only from the traditional corporate patent asserters but also a large number of NPEs, patent aggregators, and PAEs. The tactics and techniques of patent assertion and defense continue to evolve; the basic strategy has not changed.

What has changed is the size and number of NPEs, patent aggregators, and PAEs. Over the past 10 years, the number of such entities with which a company would be negotiating or litigating has increased by more than 10 times. Simultaneously, the strategy and tactics that companies use in dealing with the patent assertions have evolved. Entrepreneurs on both sides of the patent assertion business continue to develop new and interesting business models which are discussed later in this appendix.

Valuation of Patents in the Aggregation Context

Before reviewing the business models, it is helpful to understand some of the basics of the secondary patent market. At the end of the dot-com boom (March 2000), a large number of patents had been created, but the companies that created them lost control of the patents, either through sale or liquidation of the corporate assets. This surplus of potentially valuable patents, spurred a patent marketplace. Patent sales and auctions became important vehicles for shareholders to recover some of their invested money.[7] The most recent example of this is the sale of Nortel's patents for $4.5 billion.

For this secondary market to function, the pricing of patent sales has become critical and a large number of people in this new industry work to solve this problem. The first order answer to the pricing issue is relatively straightforward: The price of the patent should reflect the net present value of all the future royalty streams that the patent can generate. Once all the risks to those revenue streams are modeled, a surprising result emerges: hundreds of millions of dollars' worth of possible future royalties can evaporate into a negative net present-value price—you would have to pay someone to take the patent. The reasons for the substantial discount are numerous. Some of the risks, including the high cost of patent litigation and the high failure rate of litigated patents (around 50 percent of patents fail in litigation), greatly impact the net present value of the patent.

In practice the implementation of pricing for patent transactions is rather complex. To understand some of these complexities it helps to borrow from marketing language: a total available market (TAM) is the entire market for a product, and a serviceable available market (SAM), is the portion of the market that your company can serve. Switching to a patent focused language, there is an important difference between the total impacted market (TIM) for a patent and the serviceable impacted market (SIM).[9] The TIM represents all the revenue in a market that is impacted by the use of the patent—all of the product revenue from which future royalty streams could be derived. The SIM represents only that portion of product revenue that is licensable by a particular patent holder—each patent holder having different capital resources, skill sets, existing licenses, and risk tolerance resulting in a unique SIM for that holder. For example, the TIM may include a few large companies, a few mid-sized companies and many small companies. The patent holder may have existing licenses with some of those large companies, while the small companies are too small to bother with for a patent license. Only the remaining large companies and the mid-sized companies make up the SIM. Put differently, the revenue that cannot be achieved by the patent holder is taken out of the TIM to calculate the SIM for that patent holder. The people who specialize in patent pricing are capable of analyzing the TIM and SIMs to become deft at pricing patents.[10]

Without understanding the SIMs, the difference between what a seller will sell for and what a buyer is willing to pay can be irreconcilable. A buyer of a patent needs to understand their specific SIM in order to price a patent. Similarly, a seller needs to understand each potential buyer's SIM. Sellers that focus only on TIMs are often disappointed in the bids they receive. SIMs are typically much lower than TIMs and profoundly impact the price of a patent.

The point is that the price of the patent is correlated with *all* of the future royalty streams for that specific patent holder (or purchaser). Each of the business models described below values and selects patents for development or purchase based on the SIM for the company implementing that specific business model.

The next section describes some of the old and new models, the motivations, and the companies operating in the new space of patent assertion, aggregation, and monetization. Not all entities limit themselves to a single model, but it is helpful to think about the motivation of each of these types of businesses and how each patent holder receives value from its business model.

Classification Based on Business Model

AssertCo

- Model: Buy patents, assert them, collect royalties, distribute royalties to investors.
- Examples: Acacia, Altitude, General Patent Corporation, and many others.

AssertCo has the business model of a typical PAE. AssertCo purchases patents for assertion against third parties. The purchase may be direct or indirect. Direct patent purchases involve upfront payment for access to the patents sometimes with a backend payment to the prior owner once royalties are collected. Indirect purchases look more like investments in a company whose primary source of future revenue is expected to be from patent royalties. There are variations on AssertCo's business model, including: moving groups of patent assets into holding companies that investors can invest in; investors directly investing in the original company for the purpose of then asserting their patents; and an exclusive license being granted rather than outright patent purchase.[11]

AssertCo is typically willing to pay the risk-adjusted price of the future royalty streams from the SIM, minus profit for AssertCo. Successful AssertCos have developed skills in efficiently assessing the appropriate price of the patents, market analysis, patent licensing, and litigation.

Examples of AssertCo's include Acacia Research, Altitude Capital Partners, and General Patent Corporation. All either directly hold patents or invest in companies with patents. Each takes a revenue share (or equity) of any future royalties.

LicenseCo

- Model: Create the patent but not directly manufacture the goods containing the patented invention.
- Examples: PARC, Rambus, Tessera, and universities and research organizations (e.g., CSIRO).

LicenseCo invents the technology from which the patents are derived. LicenseCo does not directly manufacture the patented items but licenses others to produce the items. This model relies upon the LicenseCo's research and engineering skills to create new and compelling technologies. LicenseCo typically does not have the skills and capital to build and market the end product. This looks very much like a technology licensing model, and that is generally the preferred way in which a LicenseCo brings its technology to market. However, patent assertion is often part of LicenseCo's model. This is particularly true when the underlying technology is adopted much more widely than LicenseCo can license through its own technology transfer capabilities.

LicenseCo receives royalties in two ways. First, the technology transfers result in a royalty payment to LicenseCo. For example,

LicenseCo may receive a fixed amount per integrated circuit produced that uses the licensed technology. Second, where LicenseCo does not have a technology transfer license agreement in place, LicenseCo may also receive a royalty for every use of the patent inventions. For example, the patent royalty can be a per-integrated-circuit fee, a one-time flat fee, or an annual fee. The ability of LicenseCo to collect royalties in two ways enables LicenseCo to capture a large part of the TIM.

Examples of these kinds of companies are PARC, Rambus, Tessera, and universities and research organizations (e.g., CSIRO).

GroupCo

- Model: Aggregate patents, license them as a group, and distribute the royalties. Investors may practice the patents.
- Examples: ContentGuard, MPEG-LA, Sisvel.

GroupCo aggregates patents from a number of companies to form a licensing organization whose primary asset is the right to license the patents. The motivation for this model is that it is much simpler and cheaper to allow the licensing organization to license a company's patents than to try to do this itself. That is, from a participant's perspective, GroupCo is more efficient than having each participant license each prospective licensee individually. The participants share in any royalties, often as a percentage of their contributions to the GroupCo patents.

Though a participant's effective royalty rate may be smaller than they would have otherwise been able to achieve, participants benefit in other ways. GroupCo typically increases the SIM because GroupCo's primary focus is on licensing the portfolio and GroupCo's licensing efforts are not disrupted by the individual patent licenses and business activities of the participants.[12]

Importantly, GroupCo removes some of the risk of patent counterassertion for GroupCo participants (where a company is threatened with a patent assertion, it will often look to its own patent portfolio to counterassert). A GroupCo participant may have an equity stake in the licensing organization or a share of revenue from GroupCo, allowing the participant to claim some distance from GroupCo's patent assertions. Additionally, GroupCo can assert patents outside of the influence of the participants' organizations individual business strategies.

For example, MPEG-LA is one of the older and more successful of these organizations. MPEG-LA has aggregated, and licenses as a block, patents from a number of corporations. MPEG-LA licenses patents relating to the MPEG standards, including digital music and video compression used in computers, TVs, and mobile phones. Other examples of GroupCo include ContentGuard, digital rights management, and Sisvel, a European licensing entity for patents related to video and audio standards. Though the specific business model of the consortium is not yet known, the recent purchase of the Nortel patents by a consortium made up of Apple, EMC, Ericsson, Microsoft, Research in Motion, and Sony may fall into this model.

OpportunityCo

- Model: Purchase specific asset to address a specific problem.
- Examples: Broadcom, Intel, Juniper, Palm.

OpportunityCo purchases patents where it has identified a particular opportunity to enhance a negotiating position, improve a defensive position, or remove a risk to itself and its customers. The business model is relatively simple; where a company is faced with tens, hundreds, or billions of dollars of patent liability, then purchasing patents for millions of dollars to reduce or eliminate that risk is simply good business. The purchaser may also keep the patents for future risk reduction. OpportunityCo is willing to purchase patents based on the entire price of all the future royalty streams (e.g., the TIM), to resolve the particular problem faced. Because the risk faced is so great, OpportunityCo is often willing to pay the TIM price, even though the SIM for OpportunityCo is typically much smaller.[13]

Examples of OpportunityCo are Broadcom, Intel, Juniper and Palm. Each of these companies has purchased patents to defend itself in a lawsuit or provide support in negotiations. Each example company was successful in leveraging the patent purchases into reduced, or zero-dollar, settlements.

LaundryCo

- Model: Members sign up for the service, buy patents, license them to their members, LaundryCo releases the patents back into the wild.
- Examples: AST, RPX.

In the LaundryCo model, the entity buys patents of particular concern for licensing to the entity's members. The purpose is to reduce the patent assertion risk faced by members.

For example, Allied Security Trust (AST) has corporate members that direct the purchasing of patents by AST. AST members may participate in any one patent purchase. Participants receive a license to the purchased patents. Once all the members have participated in any one round of purchasing, the patents are then sold back out into the open market. Effectively, the patents are licensed (often referred to as "laundered" in this context) only for products of members who take the license, thereby retaining the value of the patents' other future royalty streams from unlicensed products. Because the patent is resold, the piece of the SIM licensed to the members is the only part paid for by the members.

Another example of the LaundryCo model is Rational Patent Exchange (RPX). RPX purchases large quantities of patents that are currently in litigation or are about to be litigated. Subscribers to RPX, corporations, receive a license to those patents, effectively creating a patent license laundry. RPX has stated that it will never enforce these patents. However RPX will likely sell these patents to the open market, ensuring that RPX can recoup the remainder of the TIM outside its SIM.

Intellectual Ventures

- Model: Multiple.

No discussion of PAEs would be complete without a discussion of Intellectual Ventures (IV). IV controls funds in the $5–8 billion range. The funds are primarily used to buy and license patents. Early licensees are also equity investors who participate in future license royalties.[14] With IV's patent portfolio exceeding 30,000 patents and with about 700 employees, the scale of the organization alone has changed the way people think about patent aggregation, NPEs, and PAEs.

The IV home page lists a number of services that range across the different models discussed above. At that scale, IV has the ability to implement many different models simultaneously.

- Purchasing a nonexclusive license to relevant IV portfolio(s) on a term or life-of-patent basis.
- Purchasing an exclusive license (subject to preexisting licenses) to selected IV invention(s) on a term or life-of-patent basis.
- Accessing Intellectual Property to use as defense against the threat of corporate assertions. For example, providing patents to Verizon to use in patent litigation with TiVo.
- Leveraging IV's sophisticated acquisition capabilities to gain access to inventions of particular interest to you.
- Using IV as a financing source for mergers and acquisitions (M&A), whereby IV agrees to purchase a target company's Intellectual Property to "bridge" the acquirer's effective offer.
- Creating new inventions in conjunction with IV's inventors and invention process.

More recently in December 2010, IV initiated litigation against a number of large IT companies.

Patent Aggregators: Good or Bad

Clearly there is a case for both sides of the good versus bad debate. On the investor side there is a desire to recover some of their investment in technologies and patent aggregators can help. On the other side, defending hundreds of patent lawsuits of varying quality is an enormous expense and distraction. Some thoughts from both perspectives follow.

Good

Patent aggregation can reduce patent exposure more efficiently than disaggregated patents. The LaundryCo companies have been successful because of this very reason. Also, early IV investors did very well. Not only from a monetary return perspective, but from the perspective of the massive patent assertion risk removed from the marketplace for those investors and frankly for many others that will never have to pay IV or anyone else for those patents. Similarly, aggregators may have beneficial effects for the early adoption of standards through models such as GroupCo.

Patent aggregator models range from new defensive models to PAE models. Investors and entrepreneurs are finding new ways to manage risk and return. As the free market resolves itself, great opportunities exist here (though not necessarily without some pain).

Bad

The cost of litigation and patent defense are high, taking resources away from product creation and distribution.

Pricing of patent licenses is notoriously difficult. Opposing sides are commonly orders of magnitude apart in patent royalty disputes. As an example, one patent asserter, an owner of a single patent, wanted $1 trillion from Microsoft.

Royalty stacking from multiple patent licenses can make products non-viable. Mobile phones, for example, include royalty payments in the $20–40 range; in developing countries, this royalty rate is untenable. Similarly, aggregators using the GroupCo model may overly encumber standards with expensive licensing regimes and broad interpretations of covered products and territories.

Understanding some of the factors on both sides of the debate, including how each company values a patent, helps explain some of the activities, but does not define the ultimate "goodness" or "badness" of the business models. In many respects, the models themselves are not where problems lie—instead, problems may be found in particular actions pursued by some actors in each of the models.

Future Aggregator Ecosystem Directions

This Appendix has surveyed the patent aggregator ecosystem and provided a model for understanding the aggregators' motivations by moving the emphasis from the label (e.g., NPE, patent aggregator, PAE) to the specific business models they have adopted and the economic rationales for those business models.

The ecosystem is continually evolving. However, meaningful change from the present ecosystem would require significant patent and/or litigation system reforms such as substantially changing the law of patent damages; litigation reforms such as loser pays, more rapid end-to-end trials; and stricter requirements for meeting Section 112 (written description, best mode, enablement) would all have a material impact on the aggregator ecosystem. In contrast, other proposed changes are less likely to have a significant impact on the ecosystem. For example, most of the patent aggregation models are not heavily dependent on injunctive relief so changes here may not be effective.

With the success of patent aggregation models, entrepreneurs will continue to seek to monetize patents and companies will make money by selling patents. As we move forward, we are likely to see continued large scale aggregation, implementing the business models discussed above and new models developed that we have not yet seen.

Appendix C

A Closer Look at IP Damages

Eric Shih and Rob Kramer

Proposed patent reform legislation in Congress has attempted in recent years to foist a gate-keeping function upon the federal courts; in other words, federal judges would be legislatively empowered to ensure that patent damage methodologies and supporting evidence were clearly set forth during the litigation at hand. Irrespective of what ultimately happens by way of any reform legislation in this regard, these same courts have, in many respects, already assumed the gate-keeping mantle by way of recent court decisions.

Some will argue that the courts, and more specifically the Federal Circuit, have aggressively (and successfully) achieved a retrenchment of patent damages over the past couple of years. To wit, the Federal Circuit vacated a $357 million award against Microsoft. Chief Judge Rader of the Federal Circuit (sitting by designation in federal district court in New York) slashed a jury damage award against Hewlett-Packard by more than 70 percent (i.e., $184 million to $53 million). And, early in 2011, in the *Uniloc* decision, the Federal Circuit gutted the plaintiff-friendly 25 percent rule of thumb, which served as the long-standing starting point for calculating a reasonable royalty by plaintiffs' damages experts.

Others, however, may argue that corporates, the courts, and even Congress may well be tilting at damages windmills. Massive damage awards understandably foment some fear and anxiety in corporate boardrooms and legal departments, though they are few and far between. PwC's 2010 Patent Litigation Study finds that there is no discernible trend in annual median damages awards between 1995 and 2009; indeed, these awards have ranged between $2.4 million and $10.5 million annually in this time frame. Moreover, the notion that patent damage awards have been excessive has been challenged in a recent study; specifically, upon review of more than 400 awards granted from 1995 to 2008, the study concluded that there does not appear to be "a systematic or pervasive problem of 'excessive' patent damage awards."

Wherever one stands on the issue of whether patent damages are reasonable or excessive, it goes without saying that damages more often than not drive a party's motivation to acquire, license, and litigate a patent against another; this is especially true in the case of a nonpracticing entity. The larger the "damages pie," the more likely someone will launch a patent infringement suit to secure the proverbial slice of that pie. The federal courts, notwithstanding the ongoing patent reform effort in Congress, have consummately executed a major transformation in the damages landscape by way of several decisions, each of which shall be discussed in greater detail further on.

Patent Damages

Section 284 provides that a plaintiff "shall be entitled to damages adequate to compensate for the infringement but in no event less than a reasonable royalty for the use made of the invention by the infringer." A common approach to determining a reasonable royalty is based upon a royalty the patentee and infringer would have agreed to in a hypothetical license negotiation; this negotiation, which would have taken place just before the infringement commenced, springs from the seminal damages case *Georgia-Pacific Corp. v. U.S. Plywood Corp.*, in which that court enumerated a list of 15 factor test. The *Georgia-Pacific* factors may be applied to the facts of a case to calculate the agreed-to reasonable royalty in a hypothetical negotiation between a willing licensor and willing licensee. For example, these factors include royalties received by the patentee, in the past or present, "for licensing the patent in suit, proving or tending to prove an established royalty," "[t]he rates paid by the licensee for the use of other patents comparable to the patent in suit," "[t]he extent to which the infringer has made use of the invention; and any evidence probative of the value of that use." Importantly, the *Georgia-Pacific* factors are not exhaustive nor do they necessarily all apply in each case; the parties may refer to and argue any issue that a licensee or licensor may reasonably take into account in calculating a patent's value.

Entire Market Value Rule

Generally speaking, the royalty base for patent damages is based on what is the scope of a patent's claimed invention. For example, damages for a patent claim directed to an improved mobile phone antenna are ordinarily based on the value of the accused antenna, and not the sales price of the entire mobile phone, which includes the accused antenna. An exception to this general view, however, is the "entire market value rule" (EMVR). Simply put, patent plaintiffs would happily apply EMVR in each and every case because it often increases the size of the royalty base in the damages calculation; the larger the royalty base, presumably the larger the damage award if infringement is established. EMVR can be applied "where the patent related feature is the basis for customer demand." Obviously, proving what is the basis for such demand is the critical question in an EMVR calculation. If a patent owner succeeds in this endeavor, however, he or she may recover damages based upon the entire product's value (e.g., the mobile phone) even though the claimed invention only covers a component of the product (e.g., antenna).

Not surprisingly, companies who have found themselves time and again on the receiving end of patent lawsuits have argued that the misapplication of EMVR and any resultant excessive damage awards should be curbed. In both the *Cornell* and *Lucent* decisions, Chief Judge Rader (sitting by designation) and the Federal Circuit closely considered the EMVR and the appropriateness of its application in damages calculations.

Cornell University vs. Hewlett-Packard Company

In *Cornell*, a federal district court dramatically slashed a damage award for HP's infringement of Cornell's patent-in-suit from $184 million to $54 million.[1] The *Cornell* decision addresses the proper royalty base to be used in calculating a reasonable royalty together with the appropriate application of the EMVR.

The patent at issue covered a method for issuing instructions to a component residing within a microprocessor. While the claimed invention covered "a component" inside the microprocessors used in HP's servers and workstations, Cornell sought damages on the total revenue from HP's workstation and server systems. Specifically, Cornell's damages expert wanted to testify that the jury should rely upon a royalty base including all of HP's revenue derived from sales of its workstation and servers. The court, however, excluded this expert's testimony that the EMVR of HP's workstations and servers constitute the proper royalty base because "neither Cornell nor [its expert] offered credible and sufficient economic proof that the patented invention drove demand for Hewlett-Packard's entire server and workstation market." Cornell adjusted its damages calculation by focusing instead on HP's sales of CPU bricks. CPU bricks are subsystems found within HP's servers consisting of modules (containing the accused microprocessors) along with various other electronic components. HP was found liable for infringement on this basis and the jury awarded Cornell $184 million based upon a royalty rate of 0.8 percent applied to a $23 billion royalty base.

HP moved for judgment as a matter of law to reduce the royalty base by limiting the base to sales directly attributable to the claimed invention of the patent-in-suit. In order to apply EMVR, the court required "credible and economic proof that damages on the unpatented portions of this technology was necessary to compensate for the infringement." In this instance, because Cornell failed to offer any evidence "indicating that Cornell's invention drove demand for bricks," or showing a nexus between demand for the CPU bricks and the patented invention, reliance upon CPU bricks as the royalty base was unfounded.

All told, the application of EMVR in *Cornell* was limited to a scenario where a patentee can establish specific evidence that consumer demand for the entire product (as opposed to just a component that contains the accused technology) is tied to the claimed invention. More importantly, the Cornell decision shows how a trial court can effectively don the "gatekeeper" mantle; a judge can actively decide what damages theories and evidence shall be allowed or otherwise. The only catch, however, is whether district court judges in general will take on as active a role as Judge Rader did in the Cornell case.

Lucent Technologies vs. Gateway, Inc.

Lucent sued Microsoft for infringement of a method patent covering data entry, without the use of a keyboard, into multiple fields of a computer screen.[2] Lucent asserted that its patent was infringed by a "date picker" function in Microsoft's software; this function permitted a user to select a date, which was then converted and entered into the correct format. The accused software products included Microsoft Outlook, Microsoft Money, and Window Mobile. Infringement allegedly occurred whenever a user entered a date using the date picker function. At trial, the jury found the patent valid and infringed, and awarded damages to Lucent totaling almost $358 million based upon an 8 percent royalty applied to Microsoft's sales revenue. With the addition of pre-judgment interest, Microsoft's overall exposure exceeded $511 million.

Microsoft appealed the trial court's decision to the Federal Circuit, which affirmed the validity and infringement rulings, but vacated the damages award and remanded to the district court. The appeals court found that "Lucent submitted no evidence upon which a jury could reasonably conclude that Microsoft and Lucent would have estimated, at the time of [a hypothetical] negotiation, that the patented date-picker feature would have been so frequently used or valued as to command" a payment of nearly $358 million. Importantly, the *Lucent* decision addressed two aspects of the reasonable royalty analysis: (1) the correct methodology for calculating the royalty rate and (2) whether application of EMVR is appropriate to determine the royalty base.

With respect to the royalty rate, Lucent relied upon a number of license agreements to establish the amount Microsoft paid for use of patents allegedly similar to the patent-in-suit (i.e., this analysis of course dovetails with the second *Georgia-Pacific* factor: "the rates paid by the licensee for the use of other patents comparable to the patent in suit"). Lucent characterized a number of the agreements as related to the personal computer field. The Federal Circuit, however, stated that mere "personal computer kinship" does not "impart enough comparability to support the damages award." For instance, the court observed that a $290 million, multipatent license related to broad PC-related technologies was not relevant to calculating the hypothetical royalty of the single patent-in-suit. The Federal Circuit thus concluded there was no reasonable evidence that this agreement was probative of the reasonable royalty applicable to the patent at issue. For other agreements, Lucent's damages expert testified only as to their structure and amounts. The court in turn found the expert's testimony to be "superficial," which provides "no analysis" of the agreements and therefore Lucent did not satisfy its burden to prove that these licenses were sufficiently comparable to support the damage award. At day's end, the court found that Lucent did not meet its evidentiary standard to support the damage award in view of the *Georgia-Pacific* factors:

> We are left with the unmistakable conclusion that the jury's damages award is not supported by substantial evidence, but is based mainly on speculation or guesswork . . . the jury's award of a lump-sum payment of about $358 million does not rest on substantial evidence and is likewise against the clear weight of the evidence. . . .

Microsoft also argued, as an additional ground for appeal, that the jury must have applied EMVR to arrive at a $358 million damage award and that the EMVR was inappropriate in the case. The court in *Lucent* considered whether the patented feature was in fact the basis for customer demand and determined that Lucent failed to prove that a customer had purchased Outlook because of the date-picker functionality. Absent a nexus establishing that customers bought Outlook because of the patented feature, the court found the EMVR to be inapplicable. The court, interestingly, hinted that the absence of customer demand in proving up the proper application of the EMVR could be addressed by rejiggering the royalty rate. In other words, EMVR may still apply—even where the accused product is a small component of a larger product—so long as the rate is appropriate. The court concluded that the application of EMVR in this case was erroneous because Lucent attempted to use an inflated royalty rate (boosted from 1 percent to 8 percent) to compensate for a smaller royalty base.

Uniloc USA Inc. vs. Microsoft Corporation

The Federal Circuit in *Uniloc* abolished the 25 percent rule of thumb, which for many years was the default starting point for calculating reasonable royalties. Moreover, the court continued its assault on the improper application of the EMVR, finding that Uniloc's expert failed to tie consumer demand to the patented invention and rejected the use of the EMVR in this case.

Uniloc's patent is directed to a software registration system that prevents improper copying of software. Uniloc accused the Product Activation function, which is used in various Microsoft software products, of infringing its patent. The jury found willful infringement, rejected Microsoft's invalidity defenses, and awarded $388 million in damages to Uniloc. The district court granted a new damages trial due to the improper use of the EMVR. On appeal, the Federal Circuit affirmed the district court's ruling, finding that the damages award was fundamentally erroneous by the use of a legally unsupported methodology.

The jury, in arriving at its $388 million damages award, apparently relied upon both the 25 percent rule and the EMVR. The 25 percent rule gives 25 percent of the value and profits of the accused product to the patent holder and the remainder to the accused infringer. The Federal Circuit admitted that over the years it had passively tolerated the use of this rule of thumb. That said, the court in *Uniloc* rejected an expert's reliance on the 25 percent rule as an arbitrary "one size fits all" approach. The court also held that this rule was fundamentally flawed because it failed to tie a reasonable royalty base to the key facts of the case at hand (i.e., the parties, patents in suit, and the products). Ultimately, the court concluded that the rule of thumb did not meet the *Daubert* standard and Uniloc failed to meet its burden because the expert's use of the rule bore no relationship to the facts at hand.

Uniloc's expert also used the EMVR to confirm the reasonableness of his proposed damages award of $565 million; that is, he "checked" his award by finding that it represented only a 2.9 percent royalty based upon the accused products' gross revenue of roughly $19 billion. Uniloc's expert concluded that a 2.9 percent royalty fell well within the range of reasonable royalty rates for software. The Federal Circuit rejected the expert's use of the EMVR as a "check" because Uniloc did not prove that the patented feature is the basis for customer demand of the infringing product. "The entire market value rule allows a patentee to assess damages based on the entire market value of the accused product only where the patented feature creates the 'basis for customer demand' or 'substantially create[s] the value of the component parts.'"

The Road Ahead

The *Cornell, Lucent,* and *Uniloc* decisions make abundantly clear that the federal courts and, specifically the Federal Circuit, have assumed a far more active (or, some might say, activist) role in reviewing damage awards and setting forth rigorous evidentiary requirements for proving up these awards. The Federal Circuit has reemphasized that for the EMVR to apply, the patent-related feature must serve as the basis for customer demand. Moreover, only those license agreements that are truly probative of the reasonable royalty for a patent-in-suit will support the damage award the plaintiff seeks. And, finally, the 25 percent rule of thumb has been rejected and is now arguably dead.

Going forward, it is quite possible that consumer surveys directed to whether consumer demand is directly linked to the patented invention shall become the *de rigueur* practice in patent litigation. Bringing aboard damages experts further upstream in the lawsuit (say, early in discovery) may also become customary as well, given the importance of identifying and securing the appropriate evidence to establish consumer demand. In sum, with the recent damages decisions discussed herein, as Congress attempts once again to pass patent reform legislation in 2011, it may well be better served to focus its attention on aspects of patent reform other than patent damages. The Federal Circuit has already taken matters into its own hands.

Notes

Chapter 1   Introduction

1. For background on the ICM Gathering, founded in 1995, see http://gathering2 .wordpress.com/suzanne-harrison/. See also Patrick Sullivan and Suzanne S. Harrison, "IP and Business: Managing IP as a Set of Business Assets," *WIPO Magazine* (February 2008). *WIPO Magazine* is the official journal of the World Intellectual Property Association. Accessed June 5, 2011, at www.wipo.int/ wipo_magazine/en/2008/01/article_0008.html.

2. See Lee Bader et al., "Cloud Computing Synopsis and Recommendation" (May 2011), U.S. Department of Commerce. Accessed June 5, 2011, at http:// csrc.nist.gov/publications/drafts/800-146/Draft-NIST-SP800-146.pdf.

3. In January 2007, the United States Patent and Trademark Office implemented a procedure for direct electronic priority document exchange with participating foreign intellectual property offices. Effective April 20, 2009, the World Intellectual Property Organization became the fourth foreign intellectual property office to participate in the PDX system. Accessed June 5, 2011, at www.uspto.gov/patents/process/file/pdx/pdx_index.jsp.

4. D. Teece, "Profiting from Technological Innovation: Implications for Integration, Collaboration, Licensing and Public Policy," *Research Policy* 15 (1986): 285–305.

5. For a more comprehensive history of the evolution of IP management see P. Sullivan,, *Value-Driven Intellectual Capital: How to Convert Intangible Corporate Assets into Market Value* (New York: John Wiley & Sons, 2000), 238–245.

6. Dr. Blair's method assumes that the difference between the market value of a firm and its tangible assets must be the value of the firm's intangibles. But is it? We suspect there are more components to this difference than may have been considered in her analysis. For example, one element of this difference may involve investor expectations, investor confidence in the CEO and the management team, and other factors that are outside of the company's set of intangible assets. While we applaud her early efforts to measure this ethereal set of assets, a credible method for measuring them has yet to be devised.

7. For an explanation of why Dr. Blair's method is appealing and why it is flawed, see P. Sullivan and A. Wurzer, "Ten Myths about IP Value and IP Valuation—Busted," *IAM Magazine* (May–June, 2009): 39–43.

8. *The Papers of Thomas Edison: The Wizard of Menlo Park*, ed. Paul B. Israel, Keith A. Nier, and Louis Carlat (Baltimore/London: Johns Hopkins University Press, 1998), pp. 844–850.

9. From encyclopedia.com, under Edison, Thomas Alva.

10. For the Enhanced Business Reporting Framework, see www.aicpa.org/InterestAreas/AccountingAndAuditing/Resources/EBR/Pages/EBRFramework.aspx.

11. For a discussion of intangible assets as a cornerstone of value, see Robert A. G. Monks and Alexandra R. Lajoux, *Corporate Valuation for Portfolio Investment: Analyzing Assets, Cash Flow, Earnings, Stock Price, Governance, and Special Situations* (Hoboken, NJ: John Wiley & Sons/Bloomberg, 2011).

12. In companies with more than one Business Unit, it is not uncommon to find each BU operating at a different Edison Level than others.

13. In this case, the term *competitor* refers not only to business competitors but also to competitors in other industries who may be considered "technology" competitors.

Chapter 2

1. For a more complete discussion of the varieties of NPEs and similar material, see Appendix C.

2. John R. Allison, Mark A. Lemley, and J. H. Walker, "Extreme Value or Trolls on Top? The Characteristics of the Most Litigated Patents," *University of Pennsylvania Law Review* 158, no. 1 (December, 2009); Stanford Public Law Working Paper No. 1407796. Available at SSRN: http://ssrn.com/abstract=1407796.

3. "Research in Motion and NTP Sign Definitive Settlement Agreement to End Litigation." Accessed June 9, 2011, at http://press.rim.com/release.jsp? id=981. See also Patentlawblog at http://patentlaw.typepad.com/patent/ 2005/01/canada_challeng.html. Accessed June 9, 2011.

4. America Invents Act Report, re "the bill (H.R. 1249) to amend title 35, United States Code, to provide for patent reform, having considered the same, reports favorably thereon with an amendment and recommends that the bill as amended do pass." www.gpo.gov/fdsys/pkg/CRPT-112hrpt98/pdf/ CRPT-112hrpt98-pt1.pdf.

5. As summarized by the Financial Crisis Inquiry Commission, a bipartisan group in the United States, there were five main causes: (1) widespread failures in financial regulation and supervision that destabilized the nation's financial markets; (2) failures of corporate governance and risk management at many systemically important financial institutions; (3) a combination of excessive borrowing, risky investments, and lack of transparency in the financial system; (4) a government that failed as a watch dog and then was ill-prepared and inconsistent in its response to the crisis, adding to uncertainty and panic in the financial markets; and (5) a systemic breakdown in accountability and ethics. A minority report for the group highlighted the failings of government regulations prior to the crisis. www.gpoaccess.gov/fcic/fcic.pdf.

Chapter 3

1. Five terabits = 5000 gigabytes. In 2005, the maximum hard drive capacity for gigabytes was 500 (in that year, Hitachi introduced the world's first 500 gigabyte hard drive, the Hitachi GST). So the employee would have to download into 10 different hard drives to download the material.

2. See the most recent *Report of the Economic Survey* at http://www.aipla.org/ learningcenter/library/books/Pages/default.aspx.

Chapter 4

1. Boeing's experience with outsourcing as a speed advantage in the "Dreamliner" case points out the flip side of the comparative advantage paradigm. Nevertheless, the front-end decision was sound and it became a matter of execution, a matter difficult to manage or control from the outside of the supplying company. This is another important lesson in the make-versus-buy discussion.

Chapter 5

1. For more information on this framework see Donald C. Hambrick and James W. Fredrickson, "Are You Sure You Have a Strategy?" *Academy of Management Review* 19, no. 4 (2005): 51–62.

2. For the complete report, see P. Sullivan and R. Mayer, "An Update on IP Reporting Practices," *IAM Magazine*, (September–October 2011): 54–59.

Chapter 7

1. See Nassim Nicholas Taleb, *The Black Swan: The Impact of the Highly Improbable* (New York: Random House, 2007).
2. John Kay, "A Realm Dismal in Its Rituals of Rigor," *Financial Times*, August 26, 2011, 9.

Appendix A

1. Stephan Ott, "Update 57: June 10, 2008," *Links and Law* (blog), June 10, 2008, www.linksandlaw.com/news-update57.htm.
2. Harjinder S. Obhi, "European Court of Justice rules in Google's favour," *The Official Google Blog*, March 23, 2010, http://googleblog.blogspot.com/2010 /03/european-court-of-justice-rules-in.html.

Appendix B

1. "The Evolving IP Marketplace: Aligning Patent Notice and Remedies with Competition," A Report of the Federal Trade Commission, March 2011.
2. As an ironic footnote to patent assertion history, Peter Detkin is credited with promulgating the use of the term Patent Troll. Peter, at the time, was the Vice President Legal at Intel Corporation. He had used "patent extortionist" to describe a PAE that had been asserting against Intel and had been threatened with a defamation lawsuit, so he changed the term to patent troll. Soon after leaving Intel, Peter started Intellectual Ventures, the largest PAE in history. Peter keeps a collection of Swedish troll dolls in his office.
3. For an entertaining read through some of our modern technological developments, see Andy Kessler, *How We Got Here: A Slightly Irreverent History of Technology and Markets,* (New York: HarperCollins, 2005).
4. The mid 1980s HP-Intel cross-license agreement was so simple and all-encompassing, it fit on one page. Two hugely inventive and successful companies cross-licensed thousands of patents in only a few words.
5. Taken from an in-person discussion with Gordon Moore, founder and Chairman of Intel Corporation and originator of Moore's Law.
6. In-person discussion with Ron Laurie, Managing Director of Inflexion Point Strategy, LLC.
7. See the public auction of the CommerceOne patent portfolio in 2004, resulting in a $15.5 million winning bid. All CommerceOne's assets had been

valued at only $9.7M. Jason Schultz, "When Dot-Com Patents Go Bad," Salon.com, December 13, 2004, http://dir.salon.com/tech/feature/2004/12/13/patent_reform/index.html. At the time of writing, the Nortel patent portfolio has an outstanding bid of $900 million and other bidders are being solicited.

8. These are not patent damages experts, but people with experience in patent development, litigation, licensing, and sales.

9. Another way to understand TIM and SIM is as the difference between a top-down vs. bottom-up market model. When constructing the TIM, aggregate numbers about a market segment or industry can be used. For example, a patented technology for a microprocessor could have a TIM including all PC, consumer electronic, and mobile phone sales. In contrast, the SIM is the specific go-to-market business strategy for the patent holder. The SIM is built from the bottom-up, beginning with the impacted product revenue of each company that the patent holder plans to approach for a license.

10. See note 8.

11. It is important to distinguish the AssertCo model from champerty. Champerty is an illegal agreement in which a person with no previous interest in a lawsuit finances it with a view of sharing the disputed property if the suit succeeds. AssertCo has an interest in the underlying assets (the patents) or equity in the entity holding the patents.

12. Each participant may have patent licenses with many companies, but because GroupCo has patents from many participants, all the patent licenses do not overlap and GroupCo will always have patents that it can license to any company.

13. The economics of purchasing patents for this reason might appear irrational, given the small SIM available to OpportunityCo. Specifically, OpportunityCo appears to be paying substantially more than the value it will receive from the patents. However, the price that patents are transacted for reflects large discounts, such that the acquisition price can often be justified.

14. Sources for IV background include www.intellectualventures.com/Home.aspx, http://en.wikipedia.org/wiki/Intellectual_Ventures, and industry relationships.

Appendix C

1. 609 F. Supp. 2d 279 (N.D.N.Y. 2009).

2. 508 F. 3d 1301 (Fed. Cir. 2009).

About the Authors

Suzanne Harrison is a co-founder and Principal in Percipience, LLC, a board level advisory firm focused on intellectual property strategy and management, quantifying and mitigating IP risk, increasing IP value capture, and focused innovation. She is also the Founder of Gathering2.0, the first online peer community for intellectual property professionals. She is a convener of the ICM Gathering, a group of 25 companies who have been meeting since 1995 to define, create, and benchmark best practices around Intellectual Property Management (IPM) and other intangibles (I-stuff). She has written numerous articles and is a frequent speaker about how companies can extract value from their innovations. She is the coauthor of *Einstein in the Boardroom* (John Wiley & Sons, 2006) and *Edison in the Boardroom* (John Wiley & Sons, 2001).

Patrick H. Sullivan is an expert on extracting value from intangibles. He has pioneered the development of methods and practices for analyzing, valuing and managing intangibles for business purposes. He is the founder of ICMG, LLC, and has consulted with over 100 companies on issues related to value extraction and valuation. The methods and procedures he has developed are taught in universities and are in use by companies around the world. He is the founder of the ICM Gathering and, with Suzanne Harrison, shares co-convener responsibility.

He is a court-approved expert on valuing intangibles and has pioneered the development of valuation methodologies specifically for intangibles, including intellectual property, knowledge, know-how and others. He has published several dozen articles on valuation and value extraction. He is a frequent speaker on how companies can extract value from their intangibles as well as on issues relating to the valuation of intangibles. His books include *Technology Licensing* (John Wiley & Sons, 1996), *Profiting from Intellectual Capital* (John Wiley & Sons, 1998), *Value-Driven Intellectual Capital* (John Wiley & Sons, 2000), and *Einstein in the Boardroom* (John Wiley & Sons, 2006).

Index